D0430468

Alphabetical Key For Quick Reference

The Vest-Pocket
WRITER'S
~ GUIDE ~

The Vest-Pocket
WRITER'S
GUIDE

Houghton Mifflin Company   Boston

Copyright © 1987 by Houghton Mifflin Company. All rights reserved.

No part of this work may be reproduced or transmitted in any form or by any means, electronic or mechanical, including photocopying and recording, or by any information storage or retrieval system without the prior written permission of Houghton Mifflin Company unless such copying is expressly permitted by federal copyright law. Address inquiries to Permissions, Houghton Mifflin Company, 2 Park Street, Boston, MA 02108.

Library of Congress Cataloging-in-Publication Data

The Vest pocket writer's guide.

   Based on: The Written word II. c1983.
   1. English language—Usage.   2. English language—
Grammar—1950-   .   I. Houghton Mifflin Company.
II. Written word II.   III. Title: Writer's guide.
PE1460.V47   1987   428.2   87-2768
ISBN 0-395-44145-5
ISBN 0-395-45403-4

Manufactured in the United States of America

CONTENTS

The Mechanics of Writing

How it is Written

HOUGHTON MIFFLIN COMPANY
Trade & Reference Division

Margery S. Berube
Director of Editorial Operations

Mark H. Boyer	Diane J. Neely
Project Editor	**Traffic Coordinator**

Pamela B. DeVinne	Kaethe Ellis	Anne H. Soukhanov
	Editors	

Contributing Editors

Rachel Lucas	Lawrence O. Masland
Bruce Bohle	Eden Force Eskin
Matthew Gurewitsch	Linda Hodgkinson

Art Directors

Geoffrey Hodgkinson	Mark Mulhall

INTRODUCTION

The Writer's Guide is a clear, concise guide to the skills necessary for using language effectively: grammar, meaning, spelling, usage, writing, and research procedures. This new edition also incorporates many features concerned with those writing problems most frequently encountered in the office and the classroom.

The first section of *The Writer's Guide*, "The Mechanics of Writing," analyzes the overall structural aspects of writing; this section provides you with the appropriate tools to use grammar and style correctly. Significant new features in this section include chapters on compounding words and writing numbers, handy lists of foreign words and phrases, prefixes and suffixes and their meanings, and a sound map for poor spellers.

"How it is Written," the second part of *The Writer's Guide* gives you various samples of styles of writing and types of written materials ranging from résumés to business letters and research papers. New features here include chapters on writing the minutes of a meeting, the format of a formal report, the preparation of an index, and proofreading. This section also includes a discussion of the planning and research required for writing an extended paper or report and an expanded guide to basic reference works.

The Writer's Guide, in short, is an invaluable reference work for all those people who wish to develop the ability to write effectively. The editors hope that the materials contained in this book will help you express yourself clearly to others.

The Mechanics of Writing

GUIDE TO SPELLING

To write correctly you must have (or find) the word. You must also know how to syllabicate it, because it is often necessary to divide the word at the end of a line. Words are divided only at the end of a syllable, and there are rules covering division for different situations that may arise.

It is always preferable to avoid division, but often this is not possible. Certain divisions are even done purposely: for example, in legal documents words are sometimes divided at the end of one page and carried over to the beginning of the next page to show the authenticity and continuity of that document.

Words are often divided according to pronunciation. Words that look alike may be syllabicated differently, and in other cases the syllabication may change according to the context of the sentence in which the words are used: for example, the words *project, progress, refuse, present, re-collect* and *recollect*.

If you do not know the syllabication of a word, look it up in *The Word Book II* (Houghton Mifflin Company) which lists most of the words you will need. If the word is not there, you should then turn to *The American Heritage Dictionary* (Houghton Mifflin).

Words must of necessity be divided in order to justify the right-hand margin of printed material: this prevents a ragged right margin and presents a pleasing and attractive appearance to a typewritten (business) letter. In the preparation of manuscript or copy for print-

ing or publication and in transcription the following
rules are generally followed and will aid you in this
preparation.

Rules for dividing words, dates, and numbers

The rules that follow are intended to offer writers,
editors, secretaries, and proofreaders a guide to traditional practice in word division. The general principles
stated here reflect conservative practices followed by
printers and publishers and not the comprehensive syllabication indicated in *The American Heritage Dictionary* and *The Word Book II*, which reflects the
phonetic structure of the word. However, word breaks
indicated here will always coincide with one or more
syllable divisions as shown in these other books.

1. Never divide a word of one syllable or a word that
   is pronounced as one syllable:

breadth	mashed	point	cough
horde	yipes	fringe	vibes

2. Words beginning or ending with a single-letter syllable should never be divided before or after the
   single letter:

   ane-mia, *not* a-nemia *or* anemi-a
   uto-pia, *not* u-topia *or* utopi-a

3. Words like *area, Ohio, ego, ogre* should not be
   divided at all, because no matter how the word is
   divided there will be a single vowel either at the
   end of a line or the beginning of the next line:

abash	idea	oozy
abet	idler	open
abide	idyll	ozone
able	iota	unique
above	Iowa	unit
easy	ivy	unite
echo	oblige	Ural
Eden	oblique	usurp
ibis	ocean	uric
icy	oleo	yeasty

4. A word with an internal single-syllable vowel should be divided after the vowel:

> visi-tation, *not* vis-itation
>
> oxy-gen, *not* ox-ygen
>
> maxi-mum, *not* max-imum

5. The preceding rule does not apply to the suffixes *-able* and *-ible* or to words in which the vowel standing alone is the first syllable of a root word. Then the division is *before* that vowel, not *after* it.

> account-able
>
> answer-able
>
> prob-able
>
> collaps-ible
>
> divis-ible

However there are many words ending in *-able* and *-ible* where the *a* and *i* do not stand alone as a single syllable. They are divided after the vowel:

> capa-ble   charita-ble
>
> horri-ble   ineligi-ble

3

When in doubt about any of the *-able, -ible* words, look them up (see page 28).

6. The following suffixes are never divided, although in poetry especially, they are sometimes pronounced as if they had two syllables. In editing, proofreading, and transcription do not divide the following:

-ceous (herba-ceous)	*-gious* (egre-gious)
-cial (cru-cial)	*-sial* (controver-sial)
-cion (coer-cion)	*-sion* (tor-sion)
-cious (deli-cious)	*-tial* (bes-tial)
-geous (gor-geous)	*-tion* (ra-tion)
-gion (reli-gion)	*-tious* (adventi-tious)

7. When a final consonant of a word is doubled in the formation of inflected forms by the addition of a suffix, the division is between the consonants:

red-der	thin-nest	bar-ring
control-ling	dim-mer	regret-ted

But if the root word ends in a double or single consonant, division is after the consonants or consonant:

fall-en	coerc-ing
confess-ing	confid-ing

When there are double interior consonants the division is between the first two consonants:

ter-res-trial	foun-tain
recom-mend	hin-drance
expres-sive *but*	confes-sion
express-way	bat-tlement

4

When *-ing*, *-ed*, or *-er* are added to a verb ending in *-le*, the division comes before one or more of the consonants, as in the preceding rule:

    gig-gled
    daw-dled
    whis-tler
    fiz-zling
    crum-bling

8. Hyphenated words are divided at the hyphen:

all-fired	window-dressing
self-control	public-spirited
strait-laced	wash-and-wear
make-believe	tam-o'-shanter *(divide at*
ready-made	*either hyphen)*

Compound words, if possible, are divided between their elements:

steel-worker	under-cover
barn-yard	over-estimate
wing-span	hail-fellow

Many words are made up of a prefix plus a word. Division is always after the whole prefix. The most commonly used prefixes are:

all-	de-	micro-
ante-	extra-	mid-
anti-	hyper-	neo-
bi-	hypo-	non-
co-	infra-	out-
contra-	inter-	over-
counter-	intra-	post-

5

pre-	self-	trans-
pro-	semi-	tri-
pseudo-	sub-	ultra-
re-	super-	un-

9. Do not divide abbreviations or acronyms:

UNESCO	FAA
WAVES	Ph.D.
OCS	p.m.
D.A.R.	D.D.S.

10. Do not divide numbers of less than five numerals. If a number has five or more digits, divide after a comma:

346,-422,898 *or* 346,422,-898   10,-000

In business correspondence numbers should never be divided.

11. Do not divide dates between the month and the day, but between the day and year in text.

October 12,   *not*   October
1984   12, 1984

In business correspondence these should never be divided.

12. The division of proper nouns follows the rules for division of common nouns. In business correspondence, however, the division of proper nouns should not be necessary and well might result in confusion or error.

13. If it is necessary to divide a proper name formed of initials and a last name, divide after the initials:

T. S.	*not*	T.
Eliot		S. Eliot
e.e.	*not*	e.
cummings		e. cummings

Try to avoid separating a name from a title:

Dr. Martin	Ms. Jones
John Martin, M.D.	Rev. Smythe

In business correspondence these should not be divided.

4. The division of contractions is to be avoided if possible. If it is necessary to divide a contraction, it should be done according to the syllabication:

should-n't
have-n't
Hallow-e'en

In business correspondence these should never be divided.

5. Do not divide years, time, temperatures, latitudes, longitudes, compass directions, or similar units.

A.D. 19	4:30 p.m.	40°28′
NNW	28°C	

Commonly Misspelled Words

Some words are more difficult to spell than others and are often misspelled by many people. These commonly misspelled words, each followed by its correct syllabic division according to the preceding rules, are listed on the pages that follow.

Word	Correct division
abscess	ab-scess
absence	ab-sence
accede	ac-cede
accept	ac-cept
acceptance	ac-cep-tance
accessible	ac-ces-si-ble
accessory	ac-ces-so-ry
accidentally	ac-ci-den-tal-ly
accommodate	ac-com-mo-date
accordance	ac-cor-dance
according	ac-cord-ing
accrued	ac-crued
accumulate	ac-cu-mu-late
accuracy	ac-cu-ra-cy
accustomed	ac-cus-tomed
achievement	achieve-ment
acknowledgment	ac-knowl-edg-ment
acquaintance	ac-quain-tance
acquiesce	ac-qui-esce
acquire	ac-quire
across	*none*
adapt	*none*
address	ad-dress
adequate	ade-quate
adjourned	ad-journed
adjustment	ad-just-ment
admirable	ad-mi-ra-ble
advertisement	ad-ver-tise-ment
advice (*noun*)	ad-vice
advisable	ad-vis-able
advise (*verb*)	ad-vise
adviser	ad-vis-er
advisor	ad-vis-or
advisory	ad-vi-so-ry
affidavit	af-fi-da-vit
aggravate	ag-gra-vate
agreeable	agree-able
allotment	al-lot-ment
allotted	al-lot-ted
allowable	al-low-able
allowance	al-low-ance

8

Word	Correct division
right	*none*
almost	al-most
ready	al-ready
together	al-to-geth-er
amendment	amend-ment
among	*none*
analysis	analy-sis
analyze	ana-lyze
aesthetic	an-es-thet-ic
announcement	an-nounce-ment
annoyance	an-noy-ance
annual	an-nu-al
antarctic	ant-arc-tic
anticipate	an-tici-pate
anticipation	an-tici-pa-tion
anxiety	anxie-ty *or* anxi-ety
anxious	anx-ious
apologize	apolo-gize
appearance	ap-pear-ance
appetite	ap-pe-tite
appliance	ap-pli-ance
applicable	ap-pli-ca-ble
applicant	ap-pli-cant
appointment	ap-point-ment
appraisal	ap-prais-al
appreciable	ap-pre-cia-ble
appropriate	ap-pro-pri-ate
approximately	ap-proxi-mate-ly
architect	ar-chi-tect
arctic	arc-tic
argument	ar-gu-ment
arrangement	ar-range-ment
article	ar-ti-cle
artificial	ar-ti-fi-cial
ascertain	as-cer-tain
assassin	as-sas-sin
assess	as-sess
assessment	as-sess-ment
assessor	as-ses-sor
assignment	as-sign-ment
assistance	as-sis-tance

9

Word	Correct division
associate	as-so-ci-ate
assured	as-sured
athletics	ath-let-ics
attendance	at-ten-dance
attention	at-ten-tion
attorneys	at-tor-neys
authorize	au-thor-ize
auxiliary	aux-il-ia-ry
available	avail-able
bankruptcy	bank-rupt-cy
bargain	bar-gain
basis	ba-sis
beginning	be-gin-ning
believe	be-lieve
beneficial	bene-fi-cial
beneficiary	bene-fi-ci-ary
benefit	bene-fit
benefited	bene-fit-ed
bookkeeper	book-keep-er
bough	*none*
bouillon	bouil-lon
brief	*none*
brilliant	bril-liant
brochure	bro-chure
budget	budg-et
bulletin	bul-le-tin
bureau	bu-reau
business	busi-ness
businessman	busi-ness-man
businesswoman	busi-ness-wom-an
busy	*none*
cafeteria	cafe-te-ria
calendar	cal-en-dar
campaign	cam-paign
cancelable	can-cel-able
canceled	can-celed
cancellation	can-cel-la-tion
candidate	can-di-date
canister	can-is-ter
cannot	can-not
capacity	ca-paci-ty

Word	Correct division
capital (*city*)	capi-tal
capitol (*building*)	capi-tol
career	ca-reer
casserole	cas-se-role
casualty	casu-al-ty
catalogue	cata-logue
census	cen-sus
cessation	ces-sa-tion
challenge	chal-lenge
characteristic	char-ac-ter-is-tic
choice	*none*
choose	*none*
circuit	cir-cuit
circumstances	cir-cum-stances
civilized	civi-lized
client	cli-ent
clientele	cli-en-tele
collateral	col-lat-er-al
colloquial	col-lo-qui-al
colonel	colo-nel
column	col-umn
coming	com-ing
commission	com-mis-sion
commitment	com-mit-ment
committee	com-mit-tee
comparable	com-pa-ra-ble
comparatively	com-para-tive-ly
comparison	com-pari-son
compelled	com-pelled
compelling	com-pel-ling
competent	com-pe-tent
competitor	com-peti-tor
complaint	com-plaint
compliment	com-pli-ment
compromise	com-pro-mise
concede	con-cede
conceivable	con-ceiv-able
concern	con-cern
concession	con-ces-sion
concurred	con-curred
concurrence	con-cur-rence

Word	Correct division
condemn	con-demn
condescend	con-de-scend
conference	con-fer-ence
confident	con-fi-dent
confidential	con-fi-den-tial
congratulate	con-gratu-late
conscience	con-science
conscientious	con-sci-en-tious
conscious	con-scious
consensus	con-sen-sus
consequence	con-se-quence
consequently	con-se-quent-ly
consignment	con-sign-ment
consistent	con-sis-tent
continuous	con-tinu-ous
controlling	con-trol-ling
controversy	con-tro-ver-sy
convenience	con-ven-ience
convenient	con-ven-ient
cordially	cor-dial-ly
corporation	cor-po-ra-tion
correlate	cor-re-late
correspondence	cor-re-spon-dence
correspondent	cor-re-spon-dent
corresponding	cor-re-spond-ing
council (*group*)	coun-cil
counsel (*advice*)	coun-sel
counterfeit	coun-ter-feit
courteous	cour-te-ous
courtesy	cour-te-sy
coverage	cov-er-age
creditor	credi-tor
crisis	cri-sis
criticism	criti-cism
criticize	criti-cize
curiosity	cu-ri-osi-ty
current	cur-rent
customer	cus-tom-er
cylinder	cy-lin-der
debtor	debt-or
deceive	de-ceive

Word	Correct division
decide	de-cide
decision	de-ci-sion
deductible	de-ducti-ble
defendant	de-fen-dant
defer	de-fer
deferred	de-ferred
deferring	de-fer-ring
deficit	defi-cit
definite	defi-nite
definitely	defi-nite-ly
delegate	dele-gate
dependent	de-pend-ent
depositors	de-posi-tors
descend	de-scend
description	de-scrip-tion
desirable	de-sir-able
despair	de-spair
deteriorate	de-te-rio-rate
develop	de-vel-op
development	de-vel-op-ment
device (*tool*)	de-vice
devise (*make, give*)	de-vise
diaphragm	dia-phragm
diarrhea	di-ar-rhea
difference	dif-fer-ence
dilemma	di-lem-ma
dining	din-ing
director	di-rec-tor
disappear	dis-ap-pear
disappoint	dis-ap-point
discipline	dis-ci-pline
discrepancy	dis-crep-an-cy
dissatisfied	dis-sat-is-fied
dissipate	dis-si-pate
distinguish	dis-tin-guish
dormitory	dor-mi-to-ry
eagerly	ea-ger-ly
economical	eco-nomi-cal
ecstasy	ec-sta-sy
edition	edi-tion
effect	ef-fect

13

Word	**Correct division**
effervescent	ef-fer-ves-cent
efficacy	ef-fi-ca-cy
efficiency	ef-fi-cien-cy
efficient	ef-fi-cient
eligible	eli-gi-ble
eliminate	elimi-nate
ellipse	el-lipse
embarrass	em-bar-rass
emergency	emer-gen-cy
emphasis	em-pha-sis
emphasize	em-pha-size
employee	em-ploy-ee
enclose	en-close
encouraging	en-cour-ag-ing
endeavor	en-deav-or
endorsement	en-dorse-ment
enterprise	en-ter-prise
enthusiasm	en-thu-si-asm
envelop (*surround*)	en-vel-op
envelope (*paper cover*)	en-ve-lope
environment	en-vi-ron-ment
equipment	equip-ment
equipped	*none*
especially	es-pe-cial-ly
essential	es-sen-tial
esteemed	es-teemed
etiquette	eti-quette
exaggerate	ex-ag-ger-ate
exaggerating	ex-ag-ger-at-ing
exaggeration	ex-ag-ger-a-tion
exceed	ex-ceed
excellence	ex-cel-lence
excellent	ex-cel-lent
except	ex-cept
exceptionally	ex-cep-tion-al-ly
excessive	ex-ces-sive
executive	ex-ecu-tive
exercise	ex-er-cise
exhibition	ex-hi-bi-tion
exhilarate	ex-hila-rate
exhilaration	ex-hila-ra-tion

Word	Correct division
existence	ex-is-tence
expedite	ex-pe-dite
expenditure	ex-pen-di-ture
expense	ex-pense
experience	ex-pe-ri-ence
explanation	ex-pla-na-tion
extension	ex-ten-sion
extraordinary	ex-traor-di-nary
extremely	ex-treme-ly
facilities	fa-cili-ties
fallacy	fal-la-cy
fascinate	fas-ci-nate
fascinating	fas-ci-nat-ing
favorable	fa-vor-able
favorite	fa-vor-ite
feasible	fea-si-ble
February	Feb-ru-ary
fictitious	fic-ti-tious
finally	fi-nal-ly
financier	fin-an-cier
foliage	fo-li-age
forcible	for-ci-ble
forego (*precede*)	fore-go
foreign	for-eign
forfeit	for-feit
forgo (*relinquish*)	for-go
formerly	for-mer-ly
fortunately	for-tu-nate-ly
forty	for-ty
forward	for-ward
fourth	*none*
freight	*none*
friend	*none*
fulfill	ful-fill
fulfilling	ful-fill-ing
fulfillment	ful-fill-ment
furthermore	fur-ther-more
gauge	*none*
genuine	genu-ine
government	gov-ern-ment
governor	gov-er-nor

15

Word	Correct division
grateful	grate-ful
grievance	griev-ance
guarantee	guar-an-tee
guerrilla	guer-ril-la
gypsy	gyp-sy
handkerchief	hand-ker-chief
handled	han-dled
haphazard	hap-haz-ard
harass	har-ass
hardware	hard-ware
hazardous	haz-ard-ous
height	*none*
hemorrhage	hem-or-rhage
hesitant	hesi-tant
hoping (*expect*)	hop-ing
hopping (*jump*)	hop-ping
hydraulic	hy-drau-lic
hygiene	hy-giene
hypocrite	hypo-crite
hypocrisy	hy-poc-ri-sy
icicle	ici-cle
identical	iden-ti-cal
illegible	il-leg-ible
immediately	im-me-di-ate-ly
immense	im-mense
imperative	im-pera-tive
impossible	im-pos-si-ble
inalienable	in-al-ien-able
inasmuch as	in-as-much (as)
incidentally	in-ci-den-tal-ly
inconvenience	in-con-ven-ience
incurred	in-curred
indebtedness	in-debt-ed-ness
indelible	in-del-ible
independent	in-de-pend-ent
indictment	in-dict-ment
indispensable	in-dis-pen-sa-ble
individual	in-di-vidu-al
inducement	in-duce-ment
inevitable	in-evi-ta-ble
inferred	in-ferred

16

Word	Correct division
influential	in-flu-en-tial
initial	ini-tial
inoculate	in-ocu-late
inquiry	in-quiry
installation	in-stal-la-tion
intellectual	in-tel-lec-tu-al
intelligence	in-tel-li-gence
intention	in-ten-tion
interfere	in-ter-fere
intermittent	in-ter-mit-tent
interrupted	in-ter-rupt-ed
intimate	in-ti-mate
investor	in-ves-tor
iridescent	iri-des-cent
irrelevant	ir-rele-vant
irresistible	ir-re-sis-ti-ble
itemized	item-ized
itinerary	itin-er-ary
it's	*none*
jeopardize	jeop-ard-ize
journal	jour-nal
judgment	judg-ment
justifiable	jus-ti-fi-able
knowledge	knowl-edge
laboratory	labo-ra-to-ry
legible	leg-ible
legitimate	le-giti-mate
leisure	lei-sure
length	*none*
letterhead	let-ter-head
liaison	li-ai-son
library	li-brary
license	li-cense
lieutenant	lieu-ten-ant
lightning	light-ning
likable	lik-able
liquefy	liq-ue-fy
livelihood	live-li-hood
loose	*none*
lose	*none*
magazine	maga-zine

Word	Correct division
maintenance	main-te-nance
manageable	man-age-able
management	man-age-ment
manufacturer	manu-fac-tur-er
manuscript	manu-script
marshal	mar-shal
mathematics	mathe-mat-ics
maximum	maxi-mum
medical	medi-cal
memorandum	memo-ran-dum
menus	men-us
merchandise	mer-chan-dise
mileage	mile-age
miniature	minia-ture
minimum	mini-mum
minuscule	min-us-cule
miscellaneous	mis-cel-la-ne-ous
mischievous	mis-chie-vous
modernize	mod-ern-ize
molecule	mole-cule
monotonous	mo-noto-nous
mortgage	mort-gage
murmur	mur-mur
mutual	mu-tu-al
necessarily	nec-es-sari-ly
necessary	nec-es-sary
negligible	neg-li-gi-ble
negotiate	ne-go-ti-ate
neighborhood	neighbor-hood, neigh-bor-hood
nevertheless	never-the-less
	nev-er-the-less
nickel	nick-el
niece	*none*
noticeable	no-tice-able
oblige	*none*
occasion	oc-ca-sion
occasionally	oc-ca-sion-al-ly
occupant	oc-cu-pant
occurred	oc-curred
occurrence	oc-cur-rence
occurring	oc-cur-ring

Word	Correct division
offense	of-fense
offering	of-fer-ing
official	of-fi-cial
omission	omis-sion
omitted	omit-ted
opportunities	op-por-tu-ni-ties
opportunity	op-por-tu-ni-ty
ordinarily	or-di-nari-ly
ordinary	or-di-nary
organization	or-gani-za-tion
organize	or-gan-ize
original	origi-nal
overdue	over-due
paid	*none*
pamphlet	pam-phlet
paradise	para-dise
parallel	par-al-lel
paralleled	par-al-leled
parallelled	par-al-lelled
parentheses	pa-ren-the-ses
parenthesis	pa-ren-the-sis
partial	par-tial
participant	par-tici-pant
participate	par-tici-pate
particularly	par-ticu-lar-ly
patronage	pa-tron-age
peaceable	peace-able
peculiar	pe-cu-liar
perceive	per-ceive
peril	per-il
permanent	per-ma-nent
permissible	per-mis-si-ble
permitted	per-mit-ted
perpendicular	per-pen-dicu-lar
perseverance	per-se-ver-ance
personal	per-son-al
personnel	per-son-nel
persuade	per-suade
petition	pe-ti-tion
phase	*none*
Philippines	Phil-ip-pines

Word	Correct division
philosophical	philo-sophi-cal
philosophy	phi-loso-phy
physician	phy-si-cian
planning	plan-ning
plateau	pla-teau
plausible	plau-si-ble
pleasant	pleas-ant
pleasure	pleas-ure
pneumonia	pneu-mo-nia
politician	poli-ti-cian
Portuguese	Por-tu-guese
possess	pos-sess
possession	pos-ses-sion
practical	prac-ti-cal
practically	prac-ti-cal-ly
practice	prac-tice
precede	pre-cede
precisely	pre-cise-ly
precision	pre-ci-sion
predecessor	prede-ces-sor
preferable	pref-er-able
preference	pref-er-ence
preferred	pre-ferred
prejudice	preju-dice
preliminary	pre-limi-nary
premium	pre-mi-um
previous	pre-vi-ous
price list	*none*
principal (*main*)	prin-ci-pal
principle (*rule*)	prin-ci-ple
prior	pri-or
privilege	privi-lege
probability	proba-bili-ty
probably	proba-bly
procedure	pro-ce-dure
proceed	pro-ceed
professor	pro-fes-sor
prominent	promi-nent
prosecute	prose-cute
psychology	psy-cholo-gy
purchase	pur-chase

20

Word	Correct division
pursue	pur-sue
quantity	quan-ti-ty
questionnaire	ques-tion-naire
quiet	qui-et
quite	*none*
realize	re-al-ize
reasonable	rea-son-able
receipt	re-ceipt
receive	re-ceive
receiving	re-ceiv-ing
recipe	reci-pe
recognize	rec-og-nize
recognized	rec-og-nized
recommend	rec-om-mend
recurrence	re-cur-rence
reference	ref-er-ence
referred	re-ferred
referring	re-fer-ring
regrettable	re-gret-ta-ble
reign	*none*
reimburse	re-im-burse
relevant	rele-vant
remember	re-mem-ber
remembrance	re-mem-brance
reminisce	remi-nisce
remiss	re-miss
remittance	re-mit-tance
rendezvous	ren-dez-vous
renewal	re-new-al
repetition	repe-ti-tion
representative	rep-re-sen-ta-tive
requirement	re-quire-ment
requisition	req-ui-si-tion
resistance	re-sis-tance
respectfully	re-spect-ful-ly
respectively	re-spec-tive-ly
response	re-sponse
responsibility	re-spon-si-bili-ty
responsible	re-spon-si-ble
restaurant	res-tau-rant
restaurateur	res-tau-ra-teur

21

Word	Correct division
reticence	reti-cence
ridiculous	ri-dicu-lous
route	*none*
salable	sal-able
salary	sala-ry
saleable	sale-able
satisfactorily	sat-is-fac-to-ri-ly
schedule	sched-ule
scissors	scis-sors
scurrilous	scur-ri-lous
secretary	sec-re-tary
securities	secu-ri-ties
seize	*none*
seized	*none*
separate	sepa-rate
sergeant	ser-geant
serviceable	serv-ice-able
shepherd	shep-herd
sheriff	sher-iff
shipment	ship-ment
shipping	ship-ping
siege	*none*
significant	sig-nifi-cant
similar	simi-lar
simultaneous	si-mul-ta-ne-ous
sincerity	sin-ceri-ty
skiing	ski-ing
skillful	skill-ful
solemn	sol-emn
someone	some-one
somewhat	some-what
sorority	so-rori-ty
specialize	spe-cial-ize
specific	spe-cif-ic
spontaneity	spon-ta-nei-ty
spontaneous	spon-ta-ne-ous
stationary (*still*)	sta-tion-ary
stationery (*supplies*)	sta-tion-ery
statistics	sta-tis-tics
statutes	stat-utes
strength	*none*

22

Word	Correct division
strictly	strict-ly
submitted	sub-mit-ted
subscriber	sub-scrib-er
substantial	sub-stan-tial
succeed	suc-ceed
succeeded	suc-ceed-ed
successful	suc-cess-ful
succession	suc-ces-sion
sufficient	suf-fi-cient
superintendent	su-per-in-ten-dent
supersede	su-per-sede
supervisor	su-per-vi-sor
supplement	sup-ple-ment
surprise	sur-prise
surveillance	sur-veil-lance
survey	sur-vey
suspicion	sus-pi-cion
sustenance	sus-te-nance
sympathy	sym-pa-thy
synchronous	syn-chro-nous
tariff	tar-iff
temporarily	tem-po-rari-ly
temporary	tem-po-rary
tentative	ten-ta-tive
terrestrial	ter-res-tri-al
their	*none*
there	*none*
thoroughly	thor-ough-ly
through	*none*
throughout	through-out
too (*also*)	*none*
tournament	tour-na-ment
tourniquet	tour-ni-quet
tragedy	trage-dy
tranquility	tran-quil-li-ty
tranquilizer	tran-quil-iz-er
transferred	trans-ferred
typing	typ-ing
ultimately	ul-ti-mate-ly
unanimous	unani-mous
undoubtedly	un-doubt-ed-ly

Word	Correct division
unfortunately	un-for-tu-nate-ly
unique	*none*
unison	uni-son
unmanageable	un-man-age-able
unnecessary	un-nec-es-sary
until	un-til
urgent	ur-gent
usable	us-able
usually	usu-al-ly
utilize	util-ize
vacancy	va-can-cy
vacuum	vacu-um
vague	*none*
valuable	valu-able
various	vari-ous
vehicle	ve-hi-cle
veil	*none*
vendor	ven-dor
vicinity	vi-cini-ty
vilify	vili-fy
visible	vis-ible
volume	vol-ume
voluntary	vol-un-tary
volunteer	vol-un-teer
warehouse	ware-house
warrant	war-rant
warranty	war-ran-ty
weather (*meteorology*)	weath-er
weird	*none*
whether (*if*)	wheth-er
wholesale	whole-sale
withhold	with-hold
worthwhile	worth-while
wretched	wretch-ed
writing	writ-ing
wrought	*none*
yield	*none*

24

Words with Confusing Endings

–ance

abeyance
abidance
acceptance
accordance
acquaintance
acquittance
affiance
alliance
allowance
ambulance
appearance
assistance
assurance
attendance
balance
brilliance
capacitance
circumstance
clearance
complaisance
compliance
concordance
connivance
contrivance
conveyance
countenance
counterbalance
deliverance
discontinuance
discordance
disturbance
encumbrance
endurance
enhance
entrance
expectance
extravagance

finance
forbearance
fragrance
furtherance
grievance
ignorance
importance
inheritance
instance
insurance
intemperance
intolerance
irrelevance
issuance
maintenance
nuisance
observance
ordinance
ordnance
performance
precipitance
preponderance
pursuance
quittance
radiance
reconnaissance
redundance
relevance
reliance
reluctance
remembrance
remittance
remonstrance
renaissance
repentance
resemblance
resistance
resonance

riddance
romance
significance
substance
surveillance
sustenance
temperance
tolerance
transmittance
variance
vigilance

–ence

absence
abstinence
adherence
adolescence
affluence
audience
belligerence
benevolence
coherence
commence
competence
complacence
concurrence
condolence
confidence
confluence
conscience
consistence
continence
contingence
convergence
correspondence
credence
deference

25

dependence
despondence
difference
diffidence
diligence
disobedience
divergence
excellence
experience
imminence
impatience
impertinence
impotence
improvidence
impudence
incidence
incompetence
inconsequence
incontinence
independence
indifference
indolence
indulgence
inexperience
inference
influence
inherence
innocence
insistence
insolence
insurgence
intelligence
interdependence
interference
intermittence
irreverence
luminescence
magnificence
negligence
obedience
occurrence
penitence

permanence
persistence
pertinence
precedence
presence
prevalence
prominence
providence
prudence
recurrence
reference
residence
resilience
reticence
reverence
science
silence
subsistence
transcendence
transference
translucence
transparence
valence
violence

–ant
abundant
acceptant
accountant
adjutant
applicant
arrogant
assailant
attendant
benignant
claimant
coadjutant
commandant
complainant
complaisant
compliant
concomitant
conversant

covenant
currant
defendant
deodorant
descendant
determinant
discordant
disinfectant
disputant
distant
dopant
equilibrant
exorbitant
extravagant
exultant
flagrant
flippant
fragrant
gallant
hesitant
hydrant
ignorant
immigrant
important
incessant
inconstant
indignant
intolerant
intoxicant
irrelevant
irritant
itinerant
lieutenant
malignant
militant
observant
occupant
pedant
pennant
petulant
pheasant
pleasant

26

poignant
precipitant
predominant
pregnant
preponderant
propellant
protestant
protuberant
pursuant
quadrant
recalcitrant
redundant
relevant
reliant
reluctant
repentant
repugnant
resistant
resonant
restaurant
servant
significant
stagnant
sycophant
tenant
tolerant
triumphant
truant
vagrant
vigilant
visitant

–ent

abhorrent
absorbent
accident
affluent
antecedent
astringent
beneficent
coherent
comment
competent

complacent
component
concurrent
confident
consistent
constituent
content
contingent
convergent
corespondent
correspondent
current
decedent
dependent
despondent
deterrent
different
diffident
diligent
discontent
effervescent
eminent
equivalent
evident
expedient
existent
immanent
imminent
impatient
impertinent
improvident
imprudent
impudent
incident
inclement
incompetent
incontinent
incumbent
indecent
independent
indigent
indifferent

indolent
indulgent
inexpedient
inherent
innocent
insistent
insolent
insolvent
insurgent
intelligent
intermittent
irreverent
magnificent
malevolent
negligent
obedient
omnipotent
opponent
patient
penitent
permanent
persistent
pertinent
preeminent
propellant
provident
prudent
recurrent
remittent
repellent
resplendent
respondent
reverent
stringent
subsequent
succulent
transcendent
translucent
transparent
urgent
vehement
violent

27

–ible & –able

The suffix –able is encountered far more frequently than its complement –ible; hence we are listing only words ending in the latter form. Both forms are entered for words that can take either suffix with an asterisk (*) next to the preferred form.

accessible	defensible	forcible	permissible
adducible	depressible	gullible	persuasible
admissible	descendible	ignitible or	pervertible
apprehensible	destructible	ignitable*	plausible
audible	diffusible	impassible	preventible or
avertible	digestible	impressible	preventable*
coercible	dirigible	includible or	producible
cohesible	discernible	includable*	reducible
collapsible	discussible	incontrovertible	remissible
collectible* or	dismissible	indefeasible	reprehensible
collectable	distensible	indefectible	repressible
combustible	divertible	indelible	responsible
compatible	divisible	inducible	reversible
comprehensible	edible	intelligible	sehsible
compressible	educible	invertible	suggestible
conductible	eligible	invincible	suppressible
contemptible	exhaustible	irascible	susceptible
contractible	expansible	irresistible	suspendible
convertible	expressible	legible	tangible
corrigible	extendible	negligible	terrible
corruptible	extensible	omissible	transmissible
credible	fallible	ostensible	vendible
deducible	feasible	perceptible	visible
deductible	flexible	perfectible	

A Sound Map for Poor Spellers

How can you look up a word in a dictionary to check its spelling when you have to know how to spell it in order to look it up? Most spelling difficulties are caused by speech sounds that can be spelled in more than one way (the standard alphabet has twenty-six characters to represent the forty or more sounds of the English language). The following chart, although far from comprehensive, will translate sounds into their most common spellings. If you look up a word and cannot find it, check the sound map and try another combination of letters that represent the same sound.

Sound	Spelling	Sample Words
a (as in pat)	ai	plaid
	al	half
	au	laugh
a (as in mane)	ai	plain
	ao	gaol
	au	gauge
	ay	pay
	e	suede, bouquet
	ea	break
	ei	vein
	eig	feign
	eigh	eight, neighbor
	ey	fey
a (as in care)	ae	aerial
	ai	air
	ay	prayer, Ayrshire
	e	there
	ea	pear
	ei	Eire

29

Sound	Spelling	Sample Words
a (as in father)	ah	**ah**
	al	ba**lm**
	e	s**e**rgeant
	ea	h**ea**rt
b (as in **bib**)	bb	blu**bb**er
	bh	**bh**ang
	pb	cu**pb**oard, ras**pb**erry
ch (as in **church**)	c	**c**ello
	Cz	**Cz**ech
	tch	la**tch**
	ti	ques**ti**on
	tu	den**tu**re
d (as in **deed**)	dd	mu**dd**le
	ed	mail**ed**
e (as in pet)	a	**a**ny
	ae	**ae**sthetic
	ai	s**ai**d
	ay	s**ay**s
	ea	thr**ea**d
	ei	h**ei**fer
	eo	l**eo**pard
	ie	fr**ie**ndly
	oe	**Oe**dipus
	u	b**u**rial

Sound	Spelling	Sample Words
e (as in be)	ae	Caesar
	ay	quay
	ea	each, beach
	ee	beet
	ei	conceit
	eo	people
	ey	key
	i	piano
	ie	siege
	oe	phoenix
f (as in fife)	ff	stiff
	gh	enough
	lf	half
	ph	photo, graph
g (as in gag)	gg	bragged
	gh	ghost
	gu	guest
	gue	epilogue
h (as in hat)	wh	who
	g	Gila monster
	j	Jerez
i (as in pit)	a	village, climate, certificate
	e	enough
	ee	been

Sound	Spelling	Sample Words
	ia	carriage
	ie	sieve
	o	women
	u	busy
	ui	built
	y	nymph
i (as in pie)	ai	aisle
	ay	aye, bayou
	ei	height
	ey	eye
	ie	lie
	igh	sigh, right
	is	island
	uy	buy
	y	sky
	ye	rye
i (as in pier)	e	here
	ea	ear
	ee	beer
	ei	weird
j (as in jar)	d	gradual
	dg	lodging, dodge
	di	soldier
	dj	adjective
	g	register, gem
	ge	vengeance
	gg	exaggerate

Sound	Spelling	Sample Words
k (as in kick)	c	call, ecstasy
	cc	account
	ch	chaos, schedule
	ck	crack
	cqu	lacquer
	cu	biscuit
	lk	talk
	q	Aqaba
	qu	quay
	que	claque, plaque
kw (as in quick)	ch	choir
	cqu	acquire
l (as in lid)	ll	tall, llama, Lloyd
	lh	Lhasa
m (as in mum)	chm	drachm
	gm	paradigm
	lm	balm
	mb	plumb
	mm	hammer
	mn	solemn
n (as in no)	gn	gnat
	kn	knife
	mn	mnemonic
	nn	canny, inn
	pn	pneumonia

Sound	Spelling	Sample Words
ng (as in thing)	n	ink, anchor, congress, uncle
	ngue	tongue
o (as in pot)	a	waffle, watch, water, what
	ho	honest
	ou	trough
o (as in no)	au	hautboy, mauve
	eau	bureau, beau
	eo	yeoman
	ew	sew
	oa	foam, foal
	oe	Joe
	oh	oh
	oo	brooch
	ou	shoulder
	ough	dough, borough
	ow	low, row
	owe	owe, Marlowe
o (as in paw or for)	a	all, water
	al	talk
	ah	Utah
	ar	warm
	as	Arkansas
	au	caught, gaunt, automobile

Sound	Spelling	Sample Words
	aw	awful, awe, Choctaw
	oa	oar, broad
	ough	bought, thought
oi (as in noise)	oy	boy
ou (as in out)	au	sauerkraut
	aue	sauerbraten
	hou	hour
	ough	bough
	ow	sow, scowl
oo (as in took)	o	woman, wolf
	ou	should
	u	full, cushion
oo (as in boot)	eu	maneuver
	ew	shrew
	ieu	lieutenant
	o	do, move, two
	oe	canoe
	ou	soup, group
	ough	through
	u	rude
	ue	blue, flue
	ui	fruit, bruise
p (as in pop)	pp	happy

Sound	Spelling	Sample Words
r (as in **r**oar)	rh	**rh**ythm
	rr	che**rr**y
	wr	**wr**ite
s (as in **s**ay)	c	**c**ellar, **c**ent
	ce	sau**ce**
	ps	**ps**alm
	sc	**sc**ene, ab**sc**ess
	sch	**sch**ism
	ss	pa**ss**
sh (as in **sh**ip)	ce	o**ce**anic
	ch	**ch**andelier
	ci	spe**ci**al, defi**ci**ent, gra**ci**ous, magi**ci**an
	psh	**psh**aw
	s	**s**ugar
	sc	con**sc**ience
	sch	**sch**ist
	se	nau**se**ous
	si	pen**si**on
	ss	ti**ss**ue, mi**ss**ion
	ti	elec**ti**on, na**ti**on
t (as in **t**ie)	ed	stopp**ed**
	ght	cau**ght**
	pt	**pt**isan
	th	**Th**omas
	tt	le**tt**er
	tw	**tw**o

Sound	Spelling	Sample Words
u (as in cut)	o	son, income
	oe	does
	oo	blood
	ou	couple, trouble
yoo (as in use)	eau	beautiful
	eu	feud
	eue	queue
	ew	pew
	ieu	adieu
	iew	view
	ue	cue
	ui	suit
	you	you
	yu	yule
u (as in fur)	ear	earn, learn
	er	herd, fern, term
	eur	restaurateur
	ir	bird, first
	or	work, word
	our	journey, journal, scourge
	yr	myrtle
v (as in valve)	f	of
	ph	Stephen
w (as in with)	o	one

Sound	Spelling	Sample Words
y (as in yes)	i	onion
	j	hallelujah
z (as in zebra)	cz	czar
	s	rise, hers
	ss	dessert
	x	xylophone
	zz	fuzz
zh	ge	garage, mirage
	s	pleasure, vision

Vowel Sounds

A, e, i, o, or *u* are often represented in phonetic transcriptions by a symbol called the schwa (ə). The schwa is used to represent the indeterminate vowel sound in many unstressed syllables. It receives the weakest level of stress within a word and thus varies in sound from word to word. The **a** in about, the **e** in item, the **i** in edible, the **o** in gallop, and the **u** in circus are all pronounced with the schwa sound. Here are some frequently misspelled words that contain syllables with the schwa sound. If you look up such a word and fail to find it, try another vowel:

absence   definite   exaggerate   humorous   privilege
correspondence   desperate   grammar   prejudice   separate

Note: The letter x spells six sounds in English: ks, as in box, exit; gz, as in exact, exist; sh, as in anxious; gzh, as in luxurious, luxury; ksh (a variant of gzh), also as in luxurious, luxury; and z, as in anxiety, Xerox.

PUNCTUATION

Apostrophe

1. Indicates the possessive case of nouns, proper nouns, and indefinite pronouns:

   her aunt's house
   the children's toys
   Keats's "Ode to Psyche"
   someone's bright idea
   one's own home

2. Indicates the plurals of figures, letters, or words used as such:

   42's and 53's
   in the 1700's
   x's, *y*'s, and *z*'s
   an article with too many *however*'s

3. Indicates the omission of letters in contractions:

   isn't   that's
   couldn't   o'clock

4. Indicates the omission of figures:

   the class of '12

Brackets

1. Enclose words or passages in quotations to indicate the insertion of material written by someone other than the original writer:

   . . . On these two commandments hang [are based] all the Law and the Prophets.

And summer's lease [allotted time] hath all too
short a date [duration]; . . .

2. Enclose material inserted within matter already in
   parentheses:

   (Washington [D.C.], January, 1972)

Colon

1. Introduces words, phrases, or clauses that explain, amplify, exemplify, or summarize what has
   preceded:

   Suddenly I knew where we were: Paris.

   The army was cut to pieces: more than fifty
   thousand were killed or captured.

   The lasting influence of Greece's dramatic tradi-
   tion is indicated by words still in our vocabulary: *chorus, comedy,* and *drama.*

   She has three sources of income: stock divi-
   dends, interest from savings accounts, and salary.

2. Introduces a long quotation:

   In his Gettysburg Address, Lincoln said: "Four
   score and seven years ago our fathers brought
   forth on this continent, a new nation, conceived
   in Liberty, and dedicated to the proposition that
   all men are created equal. . . ."

3. Introduces lists:

   Among the conjunctive adverbs are the following: *so, therefore, hence, however, never-
   theless, moreover, accordingly,* and *besides.*

4. Separates chapter and verse numbers in references to biblical quotations:

Esther 2:17

5. Separates hour and minute in time designations:

1:30 P.M.

a 9:15 class

6. Follows the salutation in a formal letter:

Dear Sir or Madam:

Gentlemen:

Comma

1. Separates the clauses of a compound sentence connected by a coordinating conjunction:

There is a difference between the musical works of Mozart and Haydn, and it is a difference worth discovering.

He didn't know where she got such an idea, but he didn't disagree.

The comma may be omitted in short compound sentences in which the connection between the clauses is close:

She understood the situation and she was furious.

He got in the car and he drove and drove.

2. Separates *and* or *or* from the final item in a series of three or more:

Lights of red, green, and blue wavelengths may be mixed to produce all colors.

The radio, television set, and records were a[r] ranged on one shelf.

Would you rather have ice cream, cake, or pi[e] for dessert?

3. Separates two or more adjectives modifying th[e] same noun if *and* could be used between the[m] without changing the meaning:

   a solid, heavy gait
   a large, high-ceilinged room
   a polished mahogany desk

4. Sets off a nonrestrictive clause or phrase (one tha[t] if eliminated would not change the meaning of th[e] sentence):

   The thief, who had entered through the window[,] went straight to the safe.

   The comma should not be used when the clause o[r] phrase is restrictive (essential to the meaning o[f] the sentence):

   The thief who had entered through the windo[w] went straight to the safe.

5. Sets off words or phrases in apposition to a nou[n] or noun phrase:

   Plato, the famous Greek philosopher, was [a] pupil of Socrates.

   The composer of *Tristan und Isolde,* Richar[d] Wagner, was a leading exponent of German ro[-] manticism.

The comma should not be used if such words or phrases further specify the noun that precedes:

> The Greek philosopher Plato was a pupil of Socrates.
>
> The composer Richard Wagner was a leading exponent of German romanticism.

6. Sets off transitional words and short expressions that require a pause in reading:

> Unfortunately, Mrs. Lattimer hadn't read many Russian novels.
>
> Did he, after all, look American?
>
> Peterson lives with his family, of course.
>
> Indeed, the sight of him gave me quite a jolt.

7. Sets off words used to introduce a sentence:

> No, I haven't seen Rowbotham.
>
> Well, why don't you do as I ask?

8. Sets off a subordinate clause or a long phrase that precedes the principal clause:

> By the time they finally found the restaurant, they were no longer hungry.
>
> After the army surrendered, the general was taken prisoner.
>
> Of all the illustrations in the book, the most striking are those that show the beauty of the mosaics.

9. Sets off short quotations, sayings, and the like:

> Jo told him, "Come tomorrow for dinner."

The candidate said, "Actions speak louder than words."

"I don't know if I can," he said, "but maybe I will."

10. Indicates the omission of a word or words:

To err is human; to forgive, divine.

11. Sets off the year from the month in dates:

September 6, 1976, was Labor Day.

Louis XVI of France was guillotined on January 21, 1793.

12. Sets off the state from the city in geographical names:

Boston, Massachusetts, is the largest city in New England.

13. Separates series of four or more figures into thousands, millions, etc.:

57,395   12,364,903

The comma is not used in dates or page numbers:

the year 1776   page 1617

14. Sets off words used in direct address:

Mr. Wadsworth, please submit your report as soon as possible.

Thank you, Emma, for your help.

The forum is open to questions, ladies and gentlemen.

15. Separates a phrase that transforms a statement into a question:

You did say you had the book, didn't you?
Beethoven's "Eroica" is on the program, isn't it?

16. Sets off any sentence elements that might be misread if the comma were not used:

Some time after, the actual data was set.
To Mary, Anne was just a nuisance.
Whenever possible, friends provide moral support.

17. Follows the salutation and complimentary close of informal letters and the complimentary close of formal letters:

Dear Patsy,   Sincerely,

Dash

1. Indicates a sudden break or abrupt change in continuity:

Well, you see—I—I've—I'm just not sure.
He seemed very upset about—I never knew what.
And then the problem—if it is a problem—can be solved.

2. Sets apart an explanatory or defining phrase:

Foods high in protein—meats, fish, eggs, and cheese—should be a part of the daily diet.
He suddenly realized what the glittering gems were—emeralds.

45

3. Sets apart material that is parenthetical in nature:

He stares soulfully heavenward—to the great delight of the audience—while he plays Chopin.
Allen—who had a lean face, a long nose, and cold blue eyes—was a stern, authoritarian man.

4. Marks an unfinished sentence:

Well, then, I'll simply tell her that—
"But if the plane is late—" he began.

5. Sets off a summarizing phrase or clause:

Noam Chomsky, Morris Halle, Roman Jakobson—these are among America's most prominent linguists.

6. Sets off the name of an author or a source, as at the end of a quotation:

There never was a good war, or a bad peace.
—Benjamin Franklin

Ellipses

1. Indicate the omission of words or sentences in quoted material:

This ended the power of the council . . . and the former regents were put on trial.
Because the treaty has not been approved by the Senate . . . it is not embodied in law.
Nor have we been waiting in Attentions to our British Brethren. . . . They too have been deaf to the Voice of Justice. . . .

46

2. Indicate a pause in speech or an unfinished sentence:

> "Yes . . . I mean . . . what . . ." she stammered.
> I thought I had better not . . .

3. Indicate the omission of a line or lines of poetry:

> Come away, O human child!
>
> . . . .
>
> For the world's more full of weeping than you can understand.
>
> —William Butler Yeats

Exclamation Point

Indicates a command, an expression of strong emotion, or an emphatic phrase or sentence:

You can't be serious!	Scram!
Go home immediately!	Bravo!
What a ball game that was!	

Hyphen

1. At the end of a line, indicates that part of a word of more than one syllable has been carried over to the following line:

> Anatole France's actual name was Jacques Anatole Thibault.

2. Joins the elements of some compounds:

> great-grandfather
> cure-all
> ne'er-do-well

3. Joins the elements of compound modifiers preceding a noun:

>a well-dressed woman
>built-in bookcases
>a happy-go-lucky fellow
>a fire-and-brimstone sermon
>a four-hour seminar
>ten high-school students
>a two-thirds share

4. Indicates that two or more compounds share a single base:

>three- and four-volume sets
>six- and seven-year-olds

5. Separates the prefix and root in some combinations:

>anti-Semite, pro-American
>(prefix + proper noun or adjective)
>re-election, co-author
>(prefix ending with a vowel, root beginning with a vowel)
>re-form, reform; re-creation, recreation
>(to distinguish between similar words of different meanings)

6. Substitutes for the word *to* between two figures or words:

>pages 6-20
>the years 1920-29
>The Boston-New York shuttle

Parentheses

1. Enclose material that is not an essential part of the sentence and that if not included would not alter its meaning:

   > In an hour's time (some say less) the firemen had extinguished the flames.
   > It was a dream (although a hazy one) of an ideal state, one in which poverty did not exist.
   > Marion doesn't feel (and why should she?) that she should pay a higher rent.

2. Often enclose letters or numerals to indicate subdivisions of a series:

   > A movement in sonata form consists of the following sections: (a) the exposition; (b) the development; and (c) the recapitulation, which is often followed by a coda.

Period

1. Indicates the end of a complete declarative or mild imperative sentence:

   > The carved ornaments on the façade date back to the fourteenth century.
   > Come home when you can.

2. Follows the abbreviation of a word or words:

Jan.	Ave.
Mr.	pp.
Ms.	Co.
Rev.	Inc.
St.	c.c.

Question Mark

1. Indicates the end of a direct question:

> What kind of work would you like to do?
> Who was that odd-looking stranger?
> *but*
> I wonder who said "Speak softly and carry a big stick."
> He asked when Harold would leave.

2. Indicates uncertainty:

> Ferdinand Magellan (1480?–1521)

Quotation marks

Double Quotation Marks

1. Enclose direct quotations:

> "What was Berlin like during the war?" she asked.
> "Gentlemen," the store manager said to the salesmen, "our first customer has arrived."
> Will Rogers said: "Things in our country run in spite of government. Not by aid of it."
> According to one critic, the conductor was "readier to persuade than to dictate."

2. Enclose words or phrases to clarify their meaning or use, or to indicate that they are being used in a special way:

> "Dey" is a title that was formerly given to governors of Algiers.

By "brace" we mean the bracket and line joining two or more staves of music.

"The Big Apple," a name for New York City, is a phrase that was originated by jazz musicians.

Supervisors are urged to "prioritize" their responsibilities.

3. Set off the translation of a foreign word or phrase:

Hakenkruez, "hooked cross," "swastika"

déjà vu, "already seen"

The Latin word *reclāmāre* means "to exclaim against."

4. Set off the titles of series of books; of articles or chapters in publications; of essays; of short poems; of individual radio and television programs; of songs and short musical pieces:

"The Horizon Concise History" series

"Some Notes on Case Grammar in English"

Chapter 9, "Four in Freedom"

Shelley's "Ode to the West Wind"

"The Lucille Ball Special"

Schubert's "Death and the Maiden"

Single Quotation Marks

Enclose quoted material within a quotation:

"To me, the key word for the American Indian is 'paradox,' " Hunter said. "The Indian's loyalty is to his heritage, but his problem is how to function in the dominant society."

Use With Other Punctuation Marks

Put commas and periods inside closing quotation marks; put semicolons and colons outside. Other punctuation (question marks and exclamation points) should be put inside the closing quotation marks only when it is actually part of the matter being quoted.

Semicolon

1. Separates the clauses of a compound sentence having no coordinating conjunction:

   The questions are provided by the analyst; the answers come from the data.

   Many industries were paralyzed by the strike; factory owners left the district, taking their money with them.

2. Separates the clauses of a compound sentence in which the clauses contain internal punctuation, even when the clauses are joined by a conjunction:

   Picnic baskets in hand, we walked to the beach, chose a sunny spot, and spread out the blankets; and the rest of the group followed us in a station wagon.

3. Separates elements of a series in which items already contain commas:

   Among the guests were Katherine Ericson; her daughter, Alice; Henry Faulkner, formerly of the Redding Institute; and two couples whom I could not identify.

4. Separates clauses of a compound sentence joined by a conjunctive adverb (*nonetheless, therefore, hence,* etc.):

> The cities that had been bombed were in ruins; indeed, they looked like extinct craters.
> We demanded a refund; otherwise we would get in touch with the Better Business Bureau.

Virgule (*Also Called* Slant, Slash, and Solidus)

1. Separates the numerator of a fraction from the denominator:

> *c/d*

2. Represents the word *per*:

> miles/hour

3. Means "or" between the words *and* and *or*:

> articles of linguistic and/or sociological importance.
> Takes skates and/or skis.

4. Separates two or more lines of poetry quoted in text:

> The actor had a memory lapse when he came to the lines "Why? all delights are vain, but that most vain / Which, with pain purchas'd, doth inherit pain," and had to improvise.

CAPITALIZATION

The following should be capitalized:

1. The first word of a sentence:

    Some diseases are acute; others are chronic.
    Aren't you my new neighbor?
    Great! Let's go!

2. The first word of each line in a poem:

    Poets that lasting marble seek
    Must carve in Latin or in Greek.

    —Edmund Waller

3. The first word of a direct quotation unless it is closely woven into the sentence:

    Helen asked, "Do you think Satie was a serious composer?"
    "For me," I answered, "he was simply amusing."
    G. B. Shaw said that "assassination is the extreme form of censorship."

4. The first word of the salutation and of the complimentary close of a letter:

    My dear Joyce   Sincerely yours
    Dear Mr. Atkins   Very cordially

5. All words except articles, prepositions, and conjunctions in the titles of books, articles, poems, plays, etc.:

All Quiet on the Western Front
"The Finiteness of Natural Language"
"When the Lamp Is Shattered"
Cat on a Hot Tin Roof

6. Proper nouns and adjectives:

Billie Jean King	China, Chinese
Bruno Walter	Bohemia, Bohemian
Clare Boothe Luce	Morocco, Moroccan
Albert Einstein	Hegel, Hegelian

Do not capitalize words derived from proper nouns and adjectives and having distinct special meanings:

china plates	a bohemian lifestyle
chinese red	moroccan leather

7. The standard names of geographic divisions, districts, regions, and localities:

Arctic Circle	Mountain States
Western Hemisphere	Gulf Coast
South Pole	the North
Torrid Zone	the South
Continental Divide	the East
Old World	the West
Middle East	the Midwest
Far West	the Southwest

Do not capitalize words designating points of the compass unless they refer to specific regions:

Holyoke, Massachusetts, is eight miles north of Springfield. Turn east on Route 495.

8. The popular names of districts, regions, and localities:

the Barbary Coast	the Windy City
the Promised Land	the Loop
the Bible Belt	the East Side

9. The names of rivers, lakes, mountains, oceans, etc.:

Connecticut River	Mount Shasta
Lake Maracaibo	Long Island Sound
Rocky Mountains	Pacific Ocean

10. Names for the Deity, for a supreme being, and for the Bible and other sacred books:

God	Allah
the Almighty	Jehovah
the Savior	the Messiah
the Holy Spirit	the Bible
the Virgin Mary	the Koran
the Blessed Mother	the Talmud

11. The names of religious denominations:

Catholicism
Judaism
Protestantism
Buddhism
the Roman Catholic Church
the Protestant Episcopal Church

the Society of Friends
the Church of Jesus Christ of Latter-day Saints

12. The names of historical periods, events, documents, etc.:

the Middle Ages
the Reformation
the American Revolution
World War II
the Battle of Shiloh
the Declaration of Independence
the Magna Carta
the Constitution

13. The names of political entities, divisions, parties, etc.:

the Byzantine Empire
the Holy Roman Empire
the French Republic
the Populist Party
the Democratic Party
the Republican Party
Democrat
Republican

14. The names of legislative and judicial bodies:

Parliament
Diet
Knesset
Congress
the Senate

the House of Representatives
the United States Supreme Court
the Permanent Court of International Justice

15. The names of departments, bureaus, etc., of the federal government:

   the Department of Agriculture
   United States Department of State
   Central Intelligence Agency
   Tennessee Valley Authority

16. The names of treaties, acts, laws, etc.:

   the Versailles Treaty
   the Clayton-Bulwer Treaty
   the Volstead Act
   the Sherman Antitrust Law

17. Titles—civil, military, noble, honorary, etc.—when they precede a name:

   Justice Frankfurter
   General MacArthur
   Mayor White
   Queen Elizabeth II
   Pope John XXIII
   Professor Kittredge

But all references to the President and Vice President of the United States should be capitalized:

President Truman	the President
Vice President Wallace	the Vice President

18. Epithets used as a substitute for a name:

    Eric the Red   the Great Emancipator
    Ivan the Terrible   the Iron Chancellor

19. The names of peoples, races, tribes, etc.:

    Maori   Bantu
    Caucasian   Ute

20. The names of languages and of periods in the history of languages:

    German
    Old High German
    English
    Middle English

21. The names of geological eras, periods, etc.:

    the Paleozoic era
    the Precambrian period
    the Bronze Age

22. The names of the constellations, planets, and stars:

    the Milky Way   Mars
    the Southern Crown Venus
    Jupiter   Polaris

23. Genus—but not species—names in binomial nomenclature:

    Chrysanthemum leucanthemum
    Macaca mulatta
    Rana pipiens

24. The names of holidays, holy days, months of the year, and days of the month:

Independence Day	Passover
Labor Day	Yom Kippur
Thanksgiving	Ramadan
Christmas	January
Easter	Monday

25. Personifications:

I met Murder in the way— / He had a mask like Castlereagh.

—Percy Bysshe Shelley

26. Trademarks:

Coca-Cola	Polaroid
Formica	Pyrex
Kleenex	Xerox

27. The names of buildings, streets, parks, organizations, etc.:

the State House
Symphony Hall
Fort Tryon Park
Logan Airport
Tremont Street
Route 91
the Free and Accepted Masons
Veterans of Foreign Wars
the New York Yankees

ITALICS

1. Indicate titles of books, plays, and poems of book length:

   For Whom the Bell Tolls
   The Little Foxes
   Paradise Lost

2. Indicate words, letters, or numbers used as such:

   The word *buzz* is onomatopoeic; that is, it sounds like what it stands for.
   Can't often means *won't*.
   She formed her *n*'s like *u*'s.
   A *6* looks like an upside-down *9*.

3. Emphasize a word or phrase. This device should be used sparingly:

   Whenever Jack made a fool of himself, he was his *mother*'s son.

4. Indicate foreign words and phrases that have not been assimilated into English:

   editors, machinists, *pâtissiers,* barbers, and hoboes

   his *Sturm und Drang* period

5. Indicate the names of the plaintiff and defendant in legal citations:

   Marbury v. *Madison*

6. Indicate the titles of long musical compositions:

The Messiah
Die Götterdämmerung
Bartok's *Concerto for Orchestra*
Elgar's *Enigma Variations*

7. Indicate the titles of magazines and newspapers:

American Heritage magazine
The New Yorker
the New York *Daily News*
The New York Times

8. Set off the titles of motion pictures and television series:

The Sting
All the President's Men
Masterpiece Theater
Upstairs, Downstairs

9. Distinguish the names of genera and species in scientific names:

Homo sapiens
Sciurus carolinensis

10. Set off the names of ships, planes, trains, and spacecraft:

Queen Elizabeth II
The Spirit of St. Louis
The Wolverine
Viking 1

11. Set off the names of paintings and sculpture:

Mona Lisa
Guernica
Pietà
The Burghers of Calais

WORD COMPOUNDING

There are four types of compound words. An open compound consists of two or more words written separately. A hyphenated compound has words connected by a hyphen. A solid compound is two words that are written as one word and express a single idea. A temporary compound consists of two or more words joined by a hyphen, usually to modify another word or to avoid ambiguity.

In general, permanent compounds begin as separate words, evolve into hyphenated compounds, and later become solid compounds. Reference works do not always agree on the current evolutionary form of a compound. The best rule of thumb is that the compound—no matter its form—should be clear in both meaning and readability (e.g., *shell-like* rather than *shelllike*). The following general rules apply to forming compounds.

Rules for Open, Hyphenated, and Solid Compounds

1. Normally, prefixes and suffixes are joined with a second element without a hyphen, unless doing so

would double a vowel or triple a consonant. A
hyphen is also used when the element following a
prefix is capitalized, or when the element preceding a suffix is a proper noun.

anti-American	American-like
anticlimax	bell-like
anti-intellectual	childlike

2. The hyphen is usually retained with *all-, ex-*
(meaning "former"), *half-, quasi-* (in adjective
constructions), and *self-*.

   all-around (*but* allseed, allspice)

   ex-governor

   half-life (*but* halfhearted, halfpenny, halftone,
   halfway)

   quasi-scientific (*but* a quasi success)

   self-defense (but selfhood, selfish, selfless,
   selfsame)

3. Certain homographs require a hyphen to prevent
mistakes in pronunciation and meaning.

   recreation (enjoyment)
   re-creation (new creation)
   release (to let go)
   re-lease (to rent again)

4. Two nouns or an adjective and noun are written
solid when they have combined to form a single
specialized term with a single primary accent. Often the meaning of the solid compound is different
from the individual meaning of each word.

bookkeeper	mothball
footnote	shoptalk

5. Nouns or adjectives consisting of a short verb combined with a preposition are either hyphenated or written solid depending on current usage. The same words used as a verb are written separately.

a breakup	break up a fight
a line-up	line up the pencils
a pushup	push up the window
a sit-up	sit up in bed

6. Compound personal pronouns are solid.

herself	myself
himself	ourselves

7. *Any, every, no,* and *some* are written solid when combined with *body, thing,* or *where.*

anybody	nobody
everything	somewhere

8. Two nouns of equal value are hyphenated when the person or thing is considered to have the characteristics of both nouns.

secretary-treasurer   city-state

9. Numbers from twenty-one to ninety-nine and adjective compounds with a numerical first element (whether spelled out or written in figures) are hyphenated.

twenty-one	48-inch floorboard
thirty-first	6-sided polygon
second-rate movie	19th-century history

10. Spelled-out numbers used with *-fold* are not hyphenated; figures and *-fold* are hyphenated.

    tenfold   20-fold

11. Compounds of a number and *-odd* are hyphenated.

    four-odd   60-odd

12. Many numerical compounds have evolved into solid compounds. A dictionary or workbook will help you distinguish the exceptions.

    fourscore (adjective)
    threesome (noun and adjective)
    foursquare (adjective or adverb)
    three-square (adjective)

13. A modifying compound consisting of a number and a possessive noun is not hyphenated.

    one week's pay   35 hours' work

14. Fractions used as modifiers are hyphenated unless the numerator or denominator of the fraction contains a hyphen. Fractions used as nouns are usually not hyphenated.

    three-eighths inch
    twenty-four hundredths part
    He ate one half of the pie.
    The pie was one-half eaten.

15. Modifying compounds are normally hyphenated, whether made up of two nouns, an adjective and a noun, or an adverb and an adjective.

    high-school teacher
    wind-chill factor
    best-dressed woman

hot-water bottle
labor-management talks
well-kept secret

However, if both meaning and readability are clear, or if the introduction of a hyphen would be intrusive, it is best to omit the hyphen.

16. Modifying compounds formed of capitalized words should not be hyphenated.

   Iron Age manufacture   New World plants

17. Scientific compounds are usually not hyphenated.

   carbon monoxide poisoning
   dichromic acid solution

18. When a solid compound noun is preceded by an adjective modifying the first part of the compound, the compound should be separated.

   schoolgirl   high-school girl
   classroom   fourth-class room

19. Compound color adjectives are hyphenated.

   a red-gold sunset   a blue-green sweater

Color compounds whose first element ends in *-ish* are hyphenated when they precede the noun, but should not be hyphenated when they follow the noun.

   a reddish-gold sunset
   The sky is reddish gold.

20. Adverb-and-adjective compounds should not be hyphenated if they follow the noun they modify.

   a much-improved situation
   The situation is much improved.

21. If the adverb ends in -*ly* in an adverb-adjective compound, omit the hyphen.

> a finely tuned mechanism
> a carefully worked canvas

22. Compounds consisting of two adverbs and an adjective should not be hyphenated.

> a very well done maneuver

23. A foreign phrase used as a modifier is not hyphenated.

> a bona fide offer   a per diem allowance

24. Phrases used as modifiers are normally hyphenated.

> a happy-go-lucky person
> a here-today-gone-tomorrow attitude

25. Compound forms must always reflect meaning. Consequently, some compounds may change in form depending on how they are used.

> Anyone may go.
> Any one of these will do.
> Everyone is here.
> Every one of these is good.

Commonly Confused Compounds

The following is a list of frequently used compounds, showing if they are open, hyphenated, or solid. If the compound you are looking for is not entered, look it up in a dictionary or wordbook. Compounds that can be written in more than one way have the preferred form entered first.

aforementioned
aforesaid
after-hours
aftertaste
afterthought
air base
air-condition
air conditioner
airline
airliner
airmail (v.)
air mail or airmail (n.)
air mass
airspace
airtight
all-around
all-purpose
all right (adv.)
all-round
all-time
also-ran
anybody
anyhow
anyone
anyplace
anything
audio frequency
audio-visual
audiovisuals
ball bearing
ballpark or ball park
ballplayer
ball-point
bank account
bankbook
bank note
bankroll
beforehand
billboard
billet-doux
birthplace
birthrate

black and white (n.)
black-and-white (adj.)
blood count
blood pressure
blood stream or
    bloodstream
blue book or bluebook
blue chip
blue-collar
blue jeans
blueprint
blue ribbon
boarding house or
    boardinghouse
bondholder
bond paper
bone-dry
bookbinding
bookcase
bookend or book end
book jacket
bookkeeping
bookkeeper
bookmaker
book review
bookseller
bookshop
bookstore
bottom line (n.)
bottom-line (adj.)
boxcar
box office
box score
box spring
brainpower
brainstorm
brain trust
brainwash
brainwashing
brand-new
bread and butter (n.)
bread-and-butter (adj.)

breadwinner
break-in
breakout
breakthrough
breakup
briefcase
broadcast
broad-spectrum
broken-down
build-up or buildup
built-in
built-up
burnout
buttonhole
by-and-by
by-election
bylaw
by-line or byline
by-pass or bypass
by-product
call money
call number
campground
capital gain
carbon copy
carbon paper
cardboard
card-carrying
car-pool
carryall
carry-over
case load
case study
casework
cashbook
cash flow
cash register
castoff (n.)
cast-off (adj.)
catchall
catchword
chain-react

69

chain reaction
chain-smoke
chain smoker
chain store
checkbook
check-out
checkpoint
checkup
circuit breaker
city-state
civil rights (*n.*)
civil-rights (*adj.*)
class-conscious
classmate
classroom
clean-cut
cleanup
clear-cut
clearing house *or*
  clearinghouse
clipboard
closed circuit
close-out
close-up
coaction
co-anchor
co-author
coed *or* co-ed
coeducation *or*
  co-education
coequal
coexist
coffee shop
cohabit
cold-blooded
coldshoulder
color-code
colorfast
comeback
commeasure
committeeman
common-law marriage

common sense
comparison-shop
consciousness-raising
co-op
co-opt
copy-edit
copy-editing
copy editor
copywriter
costar *or* co-star
cost-effective
countdown
court-martial
courtroom
crackdown
crackup
crash-land
cross-country
cross-examine
cross-index
crossover
cross-purpose
cross-reference
crossroad
cross section
dark horse
daybook
day care
day labor
day-to-day
deadline
deathbed
death rate
de luxe *or* deluxe
devil-may-care
die-hard *or* diehard
direct action (*n.*)
direct-action (*adj.*)
dive-bomb
double check (*n.*)
double-check (*v.*)
double-cross

double-digit
double entry
double-space
double time
downplay
downtime
down-to-earth
downtown
dry-clean
dry cleaner
dry goods
everybody
everything
everywhere
ex officio
extracurricular
eye opener
fairway
fair-weather
far-fetched
filmmaker
filmstrip
finger tip
firehouse
fireproof
fire station
first aid
first-rate
foolproof
free lance (*n.*)
free-lance (*v.*)
free-lancer
free trade
freewill (*adj.*)
free will (*n.*)
garden-variety
ghostwriter
good will *or* goodwill
groundwork
grown-up
half-hour
halfway

handmade	left-hand	offhand
hand-pick	letterhead	off-hour
handyman *or* handy man	line-up	office boy
	loose-leaf	officeholder
head-hunter	loudspeaker	off-line
head-hunting	lowdown (*n.*)	offset
headline	low-down (*adj.*)	once-over
high frequency	lower-case	one-piece
high-level	man-hour	one-side
high-pressure	manpower	onetime
high-rise	markdown	one-up
high-risk	marketplace *or* market place	one-upsmanship
high tech		on-line
holdup	market price	out-and-out
horsepower	market value	outbid
ill-advised	matter-of-fact	out-of-date
ill-use	moneylender	overall
in-and-out	moneymaker	overrate
inasmuch as	money order	overrule
insofar as	moreover	paperwork *or* paper work
interrelate	nation-state	
jawbone	nationwide	parcel post
jet lag	native-born	passbook
job lot	nearby	passer-by *or* passerby
journeyman	network	payroll
keepsake	nevertheless	pay-TV
key money	newfound	per annum
keypunch	newly-wed *or* newlywed	per cent *or* percent
keystroke	newscast	pipeline
king-size	newsstand	postmark
labor-intensive	newsworthy	postmaster
labor saving	nonetheless	post office
landholder	no-nonsense	postwar
landowner	nonprofit	proofread
large-scale	no one *or* no-one	proof sheet
last-minute	noontime	push button
lawmaker	notebook	put-down
layoff	noteworthy	putoff
layout	notwithstanding	put-on
lead-in	nowadays	rank and file
lead-time	no-win	read-out
leave-taking	odd lot	real estate

71

recap	short-term	time-sharing
rework	sideline *or* side line	timetable
rewrite	standby	titleholder
right-hand	stand-in	title page
road show	standup *or* stand-up	trade-in
rollback	statewide	trademark
round trip	stockbroker	trade name
roundup	stock exchange	transcontinental
run-down	stock market	turnover
sales check	stockpile	under way
salesclerk	stopgap	up-and-coming
sales tax	subbasement	vice president
say-so	subcommittee	vice-presidency
scratchpad	subdivision	view finder
secondhand (*adj.*)	takeoff	viewpoint
second hand (*n.*)	take-out	wage earner
second-string	takeover *or* take-over	waterpower
sendoff	taxpayer	wavelength
send-up	textbook	waybill
series-wound	thereafter	way station
setback	tie-in	wildlife
setup	tie-up	wind-up
short circuit (*n.*)	timecard	work force
short-circuit (*v.*)	time clock	wrist watch
short cut	time-lapse	yearbook
short-handed	timesaving	zero-growth

NUMBERS

When should a number be spelled out and when should it be written in figures? In cases in which the following rules do not apply the choice is determined by the kind of piece you are writing; numbers are customarily written out in formal writing and figures employed in informal writing (including all forms of business writing). As with many areas covered in this book, consistency of style is paramount. Whatever method you use, stick with it throughout.

1. Numbers from one to ten are spelled out and numbers over ten are written in figures:

    There are five candidates for the position.
    We received 17 letters inquiring about the job.

2. Indefinite and round numbers are spelled out:

    received dozens of angry calls
    drove five hundred miles yesterday
    a sixty-forty split of the profits

3. Definite amounts and long numbers are written in figures:

    They paid $83,000 for the house.
    She won the election by 759,323 votes.
    The pistachio nuts are $12.95 a pound.

    Numbers in the millions and above, however, are written in either figures or words and followed by *million* or *billion*:

    17 million
    at a cost of four and a half million dollars
    a three-billion dollar spacecraft

4. Two or more related numbers in the same sentence should be expressed in the same style; if one is more than ten, all should be expressed in figures:

    Today he typed 4 reports, 11 memos, and 7 letters.

    There were 25 applicants for the 12 positions.

5. Spell out numbers at the beginning of a sentence. If the sentence also contains numbers that appear in figures, you can either break rule 4 or rewrite the sentence so that the number does not come first:

> Three shipments arrived today.
> Five people applied for the 12 positions.
> We received 5 applications for the 12 positions.

In sentences beginning with a long definite number it is now generally acceptable to use figures. Many people, however, do not like the appearance of such a sentence and would prefer to see it rewritten.

> 4,500 acres were used for growing corn.
> The farm used 4,500 acres for growing corn.

6. Unrelated numbers in the same sentence should be distinguished for clarity. Figures and words can be used to differentiate them:

> In three days we sold 24 cars, 6 campers, and 11 trucks.

Unrelated numbers should not be placed next to each other. You can spell out one of the numbers, use a comma to separate them, or rewrite the sentence:

> The show consisted of 3 one-act plays.
> In 1982, 16 incumbent senators were defeated.
> There were 16 incumbent senators defeated in 1982.

7. Specific amounts of money are written in figures. The dollar sign is placed before the figure and the decimal point and ciphers are usually omitted:

   $10.95 $35 $357,928 $5 a pair

   Remember that indefinite numbers are spelled out; it is only in such cases that the word "dollar(s)" is used after the number (rather than the dollar sign before):

   spent about twenty dollars at the market.
   a forty- to fifty-dollar repair job.

   Sums under a dollar are usually expressed in figures, but it is not uncommon to see sums spelled out in formal writing. The word cents is used following the words or figures in printing and formal writing; the cents sign is used in informal writing:

   35¢   35 cents   thirty-five cents

   Remember, however, that consistency would demand:

   One item cost $1.25 and the other is $.69.

   In legal documents sums are given in both words and figures:

   sold at a price of five hundred dollars ($500)

8. Fractions standing alone are spelled out; if used as adjectives they must be hyphenated, if used as nouns they are open compounds:

   received a two-thirds share
   bought one third of a pound

   Fractions in mixed numbers are expressed in

figures; a space separates the whole number from the fraction, and a diagonal line separates the parts of the fraction:

3 1/2   20 7/8   9 2/3

9. When writing dates in which the day precedes the month, the date should be expressed in ordinal numbers or spelled out:

> I met with her on the 6th of May.
> We will see them again on the twelfth of July.

When the date follows the month regular figures are used:

> They are arriving on August 21.
> She was born on January 14, 1950.

In formal writing numbers applying to years, decades, and centuries are spelled out:

> nineteen hundred and eighty-three
> growing up in the sixties
> the seventeenth century

In informal writing figures are often used, and if the date is abbreviated an apostrophe is used to show the part that has been left out:

> John Kennedy was elected President in 1960.
> a novel first published in the 1920's.
> I haven't seen him since '73.

10. Street names above ten are expressed in ordinal figures (in this case two numbers can be placed next to one another):

> My address is 60 31st Street.

You only need to use *st, nd, rd* or *th* if a numbered street is not preceded by either East or West:

Her office is at 105 West 12 Street.

11. In formal writing the time of day is spelled out and used with o'clock. In informal writing figures are used with a.m. and p.m. and occasionally with o'clock:

The wedding reception will be held from eight o'clock to twelve o'clock.

Business hours are from 9:30 a.m. to 5 p.m.

Orders will be taken beginning at 10 o'clock.

12. Figures are used to express exact dimensions, sizes, measurements, and temperatures:

The painting measures 2 by 4 feet.

(Note that × for by and ″ and ′ for inches and feet are used only in technical writing.)

A mile equals 1,760 yards or 5,280 feet.

At birth the baby weighed 6 pounds 7 ounces.

The high today was 82 degrees Fahrenheit.

13. Percentages are expressed in figures followed by the word percent:

received a 10 percent discount.

BASIC RULES OF STANDARD ENGLISH GRAMMAR

What is Grammar?

Grammar is a system of basic rules by which the words in a language are structured and arranged in sentences. Grammar deals with rules for word order, verb forms, plural and singular noun forms, and parts of speech, among other topics.

Virtually everybody who has heard English spoken from birth has learned *basic* English grammar. But not everybody has learned *standard* English grammar: the set of rules that govern what is generally considered to be "good" or "correct" grammar.

Some specific points of grammar present problems for many people whose native language is English. This section deals in particular with those points. Areas of difficulty are examined, and the reasons for difficulty are cited.

Traditional and New Grammar

The second half of the twentieth century has witnessed a change in the way grammarians discuss grammar. Grammarians have begun to use new terms for certain classes of words. At the same time, other people have retained the traditional terms for these classes of words. The difference in classifying words does not make a difference in the way words are actually used. The way words operate in sentences have not substantially changed.

Verbs

English verb forms are fairly simple when you compare them with verb forms in many other languages. The *present tense* of most verbs has only two forms, as illustrated by the verb "walk":

Singular	Plural	
I walk	we walk	**first person**
you walk	you walk	**second person**
he, she, it walks	they walk	**third person**

The two forms are *walk* and *walks*. The form *walks* is used only for the third-person singular. *He, she,* or *it* may be replaced by the name of one person, one thing, one place, or one idea.

John walks.

The cat walks.

The puppet walks.

Happiness walks the earth.

One basic rule of English grammar is: *A verb must agree with its subject in person and number.*

That means that a first-person singular verb is used with "I," a third-person singular verb is used with any singular noun or third-person singular pronoun, and so on.

Some reasons people have problems when trying to apply this rule are:

1. They fail to recognize that *and* makes more than one.

John and Jane walk out on the boardwalk. (John + Jane = third-person *plural*.)

Jane and I walk out on the boardwalk. (Jane + I = we = first-person *plural*.)

2. They fail to recognize that *or* does not create a plural.

   Either John or Jane gets a paper each day. (Only one of the two of them gets the paper—sometimes one, sometimes the other.)

3. They fail to recognize the true subject.

   A deck of cards sits on the shelf. (The verb is third-person singular because *deck* is the subject, not *cards*.)

The *past tense* for most verbs has only one form.

I walked	we walked
you walked	you walked
he, she, it walked	they walked

Regular past tenses are formed by adding an *-ed* to the verb. Sometimes a final *e* is dropped before adding the *-ed* (save, saved), sometimes a final *y* is changed to *i* before the *-ed* is added (worry, worried), sometimes a final consonant is doubled before adding the -ed (nap, napped). Most of these past tenses do not offer too much difficulty.

Many past tenses, however, are irregular. Irregular past tenses must be learned one by one. Most of these are learned during childhood. When in doubt, one can learn the past tense of a verb by consulting a dictionary.

Difficulties with past tenses arise when a person:

1. does not realize that a verb has an irregular past tense.

2. knows that a verb has an irregular past tense, but does not know what it is.

3. confuses the past tense with the past participle.

The *past participle* is the form of the verb that follows *have, has, had,* or another auxiliary verb.

I have walked	we have walked
you have walked	you have walked
he, she, it has walked	they have walked

Notice that for *walk* the past participle, *walked,* is the same as the past tense. This is true for all regular verbs. It is even true for some irregular verbs. But it is not true for *all* verbs.

Past tenses and past participles for irregular verbs have to be learned verb by verb. Although there are some patterns that are followed in several verbs, mistakes are sometimes made because the pattern does not hold for all verbs that *appear* to fit a pattern. For example, "sing, sang, sung" has a pattern that is followed in "ring, rang, rung." But it is *not* followed in "bring, brought, brought." Mistakes are made because some people try to carry out a pattern in the wrong places.

Because past tenses and past participles present so many problems, it is worth noting some general patterns.

1. Some irregular verbs have the same irregular form for past tense and past participle:

hold	held	held
bring	brought	brought
feel	felt	felt
sit	sat	sat
make	made	made

2. Some irregular verbs have the same form for the present tense, the past tense, and the past participle:

hit	hit	hit
burst	burst	burst
put	put	put
spread	spread	spread
thrust	thrust	thrust

3. Some irregular verbs change their form for the past tense and again for the past participle:

give	gave	given
do	did	done
grow	grew	grown
go	went	gone
see	saw	seen

4. A few verbs change the form for the past tense, but have the same form as the present tense for the past participle:

come	came	come
run	ran	run

The English language has about two hundred irregular verbs. The faulty use of the forms of these verbs creates a great deal of the trouble people have with English grammar. The time spent looking them up in a dictionary until the irregular forms are mastered is valuably spent.

The differences between the past tense and past participle should also be mastered. Standard English grammar requires that the distinction be maintained when there is a distinction. For example,

Nonstandard	Corrected to
I done it.	I did it. I have done it.
I seen it.	I saw it. I have seen it.
I should have went.	I should have gone.
They have came.	They have come. They came.

The *infinitive* form of the verb is the form that begins with *to* (to walk, to hit, to bring, to give). Most verbs have an infinitive form. The infinitive form has several uses. It follows another verb.

I want *to go*.

He tried *to walk*.

She likes *to laugh*.

The infinitive may serve as a subject of a sentence.

To travel requires money.

Split infinitives are subjects of much grammatical discussion. An infinitive is said to be split when a word or a group of words is placed between "to" and the rest of the verb. Although many grammarians do not object to splitting an infinitive, a few do.

He had *to* hastily *wrap* the package.

may be changed to:

He had *to wrap* the package hastily.

But an infinitive split by one adverb (as in the example above) is not universally considered objectionable.

Even people who do not usually object to splitting infinitives do object to splitting the infinitive with a long string of words:

We had *to* carefully and slowly, picking out weeds as we went, *make* our way through the woods.

That example is generally considered to be poor grammar, or at least poor style. It can easily be changed to:

We had *to make* our way through the woods slowly and carefully, picking out weeds as we went.

Defective verbs are verbs that do not have a full range of tenses and participles. Some examples of defective verbs are:

can	shall
could	may
will	must
would	ought
should	might

Note that the defective verbs do not have a separate third-person singular form:

I can	we can
you can	you can
he, she, it can	they can

Most of them do not have a past tense. *Could* is considered to be the past tense of *can,* and *would* the past tense of *will*. They do not have past participles or present participles. They have no future tense.

Different verbs must replace defective verbs for the sense of the missing tenses. The verb *to be* is a special case. Some grammarians do not consider it a verb at all. It is unlike other verbs in the number of forms it has and in the ways it is used.

The present tense of *to be* has a separate form for the first-person singular as well as for the third-person singular:

I am	we are
you are	you are
he, she, it is	they are

It has two forms, not one, for the past tense. Note that the first-person singular and the third-person singular use the same past tense.

I was	you were
you were	you were
he, she, it was	they were

The misuse of forms of the past tense of *to be* is a common grammatical error. "You was" and "they was" are simply incorrect.

Greater confusion exists because there are correct uses of "I were" and "he, she, it were." These forms may be used in the *subjunctive* (or *conditional*) mood. For example, the word "if," or anything that suggests "if," in the present or future may be followed correctly by "I were" or "he, she, it were."

If I were President
Suppose it were true.

The past participle for *to be* is *been*. Little difficulty arises out of the use of *been*. The most frequent grammatical lapse is the omission of the auxiliary verb.

Incorrect	Correct
I been gone.	I have been gone.
He been thinking.	He has been thinking.

A common error made with the forms of *to be* is to omit it entirely.

Incorrect	Correct
I cold	I am cold. I was cold.
He big.	He is big.
They strong.	They are strong.

Forms of *to be* may be followed by an adjective.

I am cold.
You are calm.
It is weak.
We were frightened.
The rabbit was furry.

There are a few other verbs that may be followed by an adjective. The verbs that may be are sometimes called *linking verbs*. The adjective modifies the noun or pronoun. Some linking verbs are: *appear, seem, feel, look*.

I seem cold.
You appear calm.
We looked frightened.

Verbs may be *transitive* or *intransitive*. A transitive verb has to have an object. An intransitive verb does not have an object. Some verbs are only transitive, some are only intransitive, some are both.

Transitive
He stole a pig.
She meets me every Saturday.
They towed the boat.

Intransitive
He steals for a living.
Let us meet soon.
The baby teethed.

Nouns

Nouns are either *proper* or *common*. Proper nouns are usually capitalized. In general, proper nouns are names of people, places, or certain categories of things. Trademarks are also capitalized. Common nouns are usually preceded by a definite article and represent one or all members of a class.

In English the form of the noun is the same whether it is the subject or the object of a verb.

Subject	Verb	Object
The dog	bit	John.
John	bit	the dog.

Noun plurals are usually formed by adding *-s* (book, books) or *-es* (dish, dishes) to the singular or by dropping a *-y* and adding *-ies* (spy, spies). Nouns that form their plurals in these ways are considered to be regular.

But many nouns have irregular plurals. Some plurals are irregular because they are the same as the singular (sheep, sheep). Some are irregular because they have distinctly different forms that go back to Old English (mouse, mice). Some are irregular because they form their plurals as in the languages from which they come (locus, loci). Many foreign words in the plural are now acceptable following the English rules. For example, both *cortices* and *cortexes* are now considered to be acceptable English for the plurals of *cortex*.

Irregular plurals do not necessarily follow logical patterns. We have mouse/mice, louse/lice, but house/houses. Irregular plurals must be learned individually.

Whether the plural is regular or irregular, it takes the plural form of the verb. And the form is the same whether the noun is the object or subject of a verb.

The boys hit the girls.
The girls hit the boys.

Collective nouns and *nouns that are plural in construction* often confuse people. Which form of the verb is used with "the committee," "clothes," "clothing," "army," etc.?

To some extent, the logic of the meaning has to be considered. For collective nouns like *committee, army, flock,* or *congress,* one must consider whether the members are behaving as a single unit or as a set of individual units.

Congress votes today.
The committee argue often about their opinions.
The cattle run off in different directions.
The jury is sequestered in the hotel.
The jury are fighting about their verdict.

Some nouns are constructed so that the form is by nature singular or plural.

The clothing is on the bed where I left it.

The clothes are on the bed where I left them.

It is not only necessary to have agreement with the verb; it is also necessary for any pronouns to agree in number with the noun.

Possessive forms of the noun are generally formed by adding *'s* to the singular and ' to plurals that end in *s*. If the plural is irregular and does not end in *s*, then *'s* is added to the plural form.

Singular	Plural
the dog's bones	the dogs' bones
the lady's clothes	the ladies' clothes
the man's ties	the men's ties

The same possessive forms are used when the possessives are in the predicate position:

These are the dog's.
These are the dogs'.

These are the lady's.
These are the ladies'.

These are the man's.
These are the men's.

Pronouns

Personal pronouns present some of the greatest grammatical problems for speakers and writers of English. Unlike nouns, pronouns have different forms when

89

they are used as subjects and objects. They also have two possessive forms and a reflexive form.

As *subjects* of verbs, the pronouns are:

Singular	Plural
I	we
you	you
he, she, it	they

Notice that "you" is both singular and plural; the same form is used whether one is addressing one person or several.

Most people tend to choose the correct form of the pronoun when there is only one pronoun required. (I went, he went, we went, they went.) Some people have problems when there is more than one pronoun.

Incorrect	Correct
Him and me went.	He and I went.
Us and them went.	We and they went.

A good rule is to try each pronoun separately and see if it sounds correct. That will help you select the correct form in combinations.

Incorrect	Correct
Him went.	He went.
Us went.	We went.

As *objects* of verbs or prepositions, the pronouns are:

Singular	Plural
me	us
you	you
him, her, it	them

John hit him.   Phil looked at you.
Mary fired her.   Henry gave the book to me.
Sally kissed us.   Sue sent for it.
James tried them.

Once again, people tend to choose the correct form of the pronoun when there is only one object. Some people have problems when there is more than one object.

Incorrect	Correct
John hit him and I.	John hit him and me.
Sue sent for her and they.	Sue sent for her and them.

When in doubt, try each pronoun alone. You will probably select the correct form.

Possessive pronouns that occur before the noun are sometimes termed *determiners* or *determinatives*. Whatever grammarians call them, they have these forms:

Singular	Plural
my	our
your	your
his, her, its	their

Notice that there is no apostrophe in *its*.

These pronouns are generally placed before any adjectives that precede the noun:

my dog   my big dog   my big, red, ugly dog

Possessive pronouns in predicate position or in absolute form are:

Singular	Plural
mine	ours
yours	yours
his, hers, its	theirs

Examples of the use of these pronouns:

The book is mine.

Mine is the glory.

One room is ours, the other theirs.

Yours is not to reason why.

Is it his or hers?

In modern usage, these pronouns do not precede the noun. "Mine eyes have seen wonders" is archaic usage.

Reflexive pronouns end in *self* or *selves*.

myself	ourselves
yourself	yourselves
himself, herself, itself	themselves

They are used for emphasis or as an object (direct or indirect) of a verb or pronoun.

I hurt myself.

I did it myself.

Feed yourself.

You yourselves are to blame.

He talks to himself.

She gives herself airs.

It grew by itself.

They themselves saw it.

Notice that the reflexive pronouns have different

forms for the second person singular and plural: yourself and yourselves.

There are other pronouns as well. For example:

either	each	all
few	somebody	anything
anyone	nobody	one
neither	both	some
something	someone	anybody
nothing	no one	many

People often have difficulty matching a pronoun to an antecedent. The pronoun must agree with its antecedent in person and number. But sometimes it is not clear what that person or number is.

John lost his hat.
One of the boys lost his hat.
Somebody lost his hat.

The last example is acceptable if the hat was clearly a man's hat. For many years, *his* would have been acceptable whether the somebody were male or female—as long as it was not clear whether male or female. Grammatically, "somebody lost his hat" is still acceptable. But social forces have overtaken grammatical neatness on this issue.

Until recently, *his* was the correct pronoun to use if it were unclear whether the antecedent was male or female. But with greater insistence on women's equality, people are beginning to recognize a male bias in the universal use of *his* in such situations. A good alternative has not yet been discovered.

What are the possible solutions? Substitute "his or her" for "his." Rewrite the sentence entirely. Use the grammatically improper "their."

Each is entitled to his own opinion.

Each is entitled to his or her own opinion.

Each is entitled to their own opinion.

One is entitled to one's own opinion.

People are entitled to their own opinions.

None of the solutions satisfies all the objections. But "his or her," although awkward, is gaining wide use. The sentences that avoid "each" may solve the problem, but such solutions may drive out the use of the word "each." And the meaning of the sentences are subtly altered. For the present, "his or her" may be the best of several unsatisfactory solutions.

Unclear antecedents occur when more than one noun or pronoun can logically be the antecedent.

Marie told Lucy that she had won a prize.

Who won the prize, Marie or Lucy? The word "she" could refer to either. Technically, "she" is supposed to refer to the nearest antecedent, but in practice that rule does not work well. Sentences of this kind cannot be corrected by a simple repositioning of words. The sentences must be rewritten.

Marie had won a prize, and she told Lucy about it.

Lucy had won a prize, and Marie told her about it.

Adjectives

Adjectives modify nouns. They normally are placed before the noun. Several may be grouped together.

the *blue* sky
the *clear blue* sky
the *clear, blue, cloudless* sky

Adjectives may also be placed after the verb *to be* or a linking verb.

The sky is blue.
The sky looks blue and clear.
The sky appears blue, clear, and cloudless.

Adjectives may be grouped together, or some may be placed before the noun and others after *to be*.

The blue sky is clear.
The clear blue sky is sunny and cloudless.

Most adjectives may have a comparative or superlative form.

blue, bluer, bluest
clear, clearer, clearest

Those that do not may form comparatives or superlatives by adding *more* and *most*.

beautiful, more beautiful, most beautiful

Adverbs

Adverbs modify verbs, adjectives, or the predicate parts of sentences. Many adverbs end in *-ly*, but many do not. And not all words that end in *-ly* are adverbs.

An adverb may be placed in various parts of a sentence. Sometimes the placement of an adverb affects the emphasis. If there is a customary location for an adverb, it is at the end of a sentence or clause.

The moon rose *slowly*.
Slowly the moon rose.
The moon *slowly* rose.

Trouble occurs when people confuse adjectives and adverbs. Adverbs are used to modify verbs or adjectives. Adjectives modify nouns and pronouns.

Incorrect	Correct
She sings good.	She sings well.
	(*Well* modifies *sings*.)
He is real handsome.	He is really handsome.
	(*Really* modifies *handsome*.)
The tie does not look well on you.	The tie does not look good on you.
	(*Look* is a linking verb and requires an adjective.)

Prepositions

Prepositions are words that show relationships, often between verbs and nouns or nouns and nouns.

Let's go *to* the movies.
the window *over* the door
I'll wait *for* you.

Prepositions take objects. That means that pronouns that follow prepositions should be in the objective form:

wait for *him*
talk to *her*
rule over *us*
write on *them*

The selection of the correct preposition is often a matter of custom. For example, you wait *for* somebody, if you are expecting him or her. You wait *on* somebody if you are a waiter or waitress. Many people say *wait on* when they mean *wait for*.

An old rule of grammar stated that a sentence should never end with a preposition. This rule is rarely observed. Often a sentence is made more stiff or awkward when a correction is made to avoid a preposition at the end.

Some words that are prepositions are also adverbs. The distinction between the two sometimes escapes people. Fortunately, there are few situations in which people must discern the difference. Unfortunately, some people who try to eliminate prepositions at the ends of sentences occasionally eliminate adverbs as well.

Conjunctions

Conjunctions are words that connect other words, phrases, or clauses.

Coordinating conjunctions connect equally constructed grammatical elements. These elements may be individual words, phrases, or independent clauses. For example, *and, or,* and *but* are coordinating conjunctions in the following:

I like vanilla *and* chocolate.
I do not like going to school *or* staying at home.
Father works at home; *but* mother goes to an office.

97

The main concern when using coordinating conjunctions is to make sure the elements are equally constructed.

Correlative conjunctions come in pairs: *neither . . . nor, either . . . or, not only . . . but also.*

He has *neither* the time *nor* the money for that scheme.

We can *either* go to the zoo *or* visit grandma.

Not only do I have to clean the mess, *but* I *also* have to pay damages.

Subordinating conjunctions introduce dependent clauses.

We heard *that* you were sick.

The man *who* came to dinner is my uncle.

WORDS INTO SENTENCES

What is a Sentence?

A sentence is a separate grammatical unit that conveys an idea. A sentence usually has at least one subject and one verb. A written sentence ends in a period, question mark, or exclamation point.

Declarative Sentences

Most sentences end in periods. They are declarative sentences. The simplest standard sentence has a noun or pronoun and a verb.

subject	verb
I	sleep.
He	eats.
Kittens	play.
We	tried.
You	fell.
Henry	swam.

These simple two-word expressions are complete sentences. Each has a subject and a verb; each ends in a period. In actual speech and writing, very few sentences follow this simple sentence pattern. Details are added to each part. A written passage that contained nothing but two-word sentences would be choppy, dull, and immature. But such simple sentences are useful as starting points from which to examine form and structure in longer sentences. In a long and complicated sentence it is often important to be able to pick out the subject and the verb.

Whenever I have an exam the following morning, *I sleep* fitfully all night.

subject⌐ ⌐⊐ verb

Despite heavy rains and rough weather, *Henry swam* across the lake to rescue the children.

subject

verb ⌐⊐ subject

verb

Our pet *kittens,* those fluffy delights, *play* incessantly with balls of yarn.

Direct Object

A simple *subject* + *verb* sentence, such as any of the preceding, must have an *intransitive verb*, a verb that

99

does not take an object. If the verb is *transitive,* it must take a direct object.

The basic sentence pattern for a transitive verb is:

subject	verb	direct object
I	like	you.
He	eats	strawberries.
We	played	checkers.
Henry	hit	Charlie.
You	saw	something.

The verb, the object, and any words that modify the verb and object all belong to the *predicate* part of a sentence. A sentence has two parts: a *subject* and a *predicate.*

The direct object is part of the predicate of a sentence. Notice that in most cases the word order indicates which is the subject and which is the object. The form of the word does not change. Only the position changes.

subject	verb	direct object
Henry	hit	Charlie.
Charlie	hit	Henry.
Lisa	likes	someone.
Someone	likes	Lisa.

But for certain pronouns, there is a different form whether the pronoun is the subject or the object.

subject	verb	direct object
I	greeted	him.
He	greeted	me.
She	likes	us.
We	like	her.

It is important to remember to use the correct form for subject and object when dealing with these pronouns.

Even these sentences are unusually short. There are various ways to lengthen sentences. In general sentences are made longer by adding details. Each detail makes a sentence more specific. Both the subject and the predicate of a sentence can be modified by adding details.

Modifying the Subject

The subject of a sentence is usually modified by adding articles, pronouns, demonstrative pronouns (all of which are sometimes called determiners), adjectives, and noun-modifiers. Adjectives can themselves be modified by adverbs.

Notice the way the subject of the simple sentence "The cat eats fish" can be given greater detail.

subject	predicate
The cat	eats fish.
The *striped tawny* cat	eats fish.
My striped tawny alley cat	eats fish.
That horribly fat alley cat	eats fish.

Modifying the Predicate

The predicate of a sentence can also be modified. The verb may be modified or the direct object may be modified. Articles, pronouns, and adjectives may modify the direct object. Adverbs may modify the verb itself. Adverbs may also modify the adjectives that modify direct objects. In the simple sentence "The cat eats fish" the predicate can be also given greater detail.

subject	predicate
The cat	eats *raw* fish.
The cat	eats *raw smelly* fish.
The cat	eats *that* fish *quickly*.
The cat	eats *horribly smelly* fish.
The cat	eats *the raw, horribly smelly* fish *quickly*.

Notice the different functions of the adverbs, "horribly" and "quickly." The adverb "horribly" modifies "smelly"—an adjective. The adverb "quickly" modifies "eats"—the verb.

Indirect Object

An indirect object is a noun or pronoun that names the person *to* whom or *for* whom or the thing *to* which or *for* which an action is done. The indirect object follows an action verb in the active voice and precedes a direct object. The best way to identify an indirect object is to imagine that the word "to" or "for" precedes it as you read the sentence.

subject	verb	indirect object	direct object
Tom	gave	Jenny	a gift.
They	built	themselves	a house.
He	told	Sarah	the news.
Ellen	cooked	the family	a meal.

If, however, the word "to" or "for" is actually part of the sentence, the noun or pronoun that follows it will be the object of the preposition "to" or "for," rather than an indirect object. The examples above could be rewritten to make the indirect object in each the object of a prepositional phrase, as follows:

subject	verb	direct object	prepositional phrase
Tom	gave	a gift	to Jenny.
They	built	a house	for themselves.
He	told	the news	to Sarah.
Ellen	cooked	a meal	for the family.

In each case, use of the word "to" or "for" has changed the distinctive order of the words in the sentence, which also identifies an indirect object.

"To be" and Other Linking Verbs

A few verbs do not take any objects. These verbs are called *linking verbs* and form the predicate by linking the subject to a following noun or adjective. The most common linking verb is the verb "to be" and all its forms. Certain other verbs such as "appear," "seem," "look," "taste," or "smell" may follow the same pattern when they function as linking verbs.

The chief point to note is that *the adjective* that occurs in the predicate part of the sentence *modifies the subject*.

subject	verb	predicate adjective
Joan	is	*pretty.*
John	appears	*tall.*
The cat	seems	*frightened.*
The dress	looks	*good.*
The soup	tastes	*delicious.*
The rose	smells	*sweet.*

The words in italics are all adjectives that modify the subjects of the sentences. They are known as *predicate adjectives* or *predicate complements*. It is important to recognize this group. Failure to recognize a linking verb causes some people mistakenly to use an adverb instead of an adjective.

Sometimes the verb "to be" links two nouns. Then "to be" or any of its forms acts almost like an equal sign. The noun that follows "to be" is not an object. It is known as a *predicate nominative*.

subject	verb	predicate nominative
I	am	*a person.* (I = a person.)
Eddie	was	*a giant.*
Claudia	is	*a soprano.*
The sign	had been	*a beacon.*
They	were	*the leaders.*
Allan	was	*chairman.*

The predicate nominative in each sentence has been italicized to help identify it.

Sentences Beginning with "There"

Many sentences begin with "There."

There are ten *people* in the room.
There is *hope.*
There are no *ghosts.*
There does not seem to be any *chance.*
There may be *some* left.
There was *one* left.

In such sentences, "There" is *not* the subject. The verb must agree with the noun or pronoun that follows it. When "There" begins a sentence, it usually signals that the verb comes before the subject.

There + verb + subject.

Because this is not normal English word order, writers often fall into the trap of failing to make the verb agree with the subject. In the examples above, the subject has been italicized.

Passive Voice Sentences

All the sentences so far have been in the *active voice*. In the active voice, the subject acts on the verb and the verb acts on the direct object, when there is one.

In the *passive voice,* the subject of the sentence *is acted upon by the verb*. What would have been the direct object in an active voice sentence becomes the subject of a passive voice sentence. To illustrate the difference:

Active

subject	verb	direct object
Amy	found	the treasure.
Paul	hears	the bells.

Passive

subject	verb	
The treasure	was found	by Amy.
The bells	are heard	by Paul.

Notice that the verb agrees with the subject. Notice also that an auxiliary verb is needed in the passive.

subject	+ auxiliary verb	
Phil	*was*	*seen* leaving the building.
Strawberries	*are*	*eaten* in early summer.
Unkind rumors	*have been*	*spread* about Gail.
The soldiers	*were*	*killed* instantly.
The fish	*was*	*eaten* quickly.
Linda	*was*	*interviewed* at home

The use of the passive places the emphasis on the receiver of the action. That kind of emphasis is important in many kinds of writing. It is useful when the agents performing the action are unknown, unimportant, or unidentified. The passive voice is very important in scientific and technical writing; in fact, the passive is often the preferred style. The passive voice is often important in news reporting when sources may not be named. It is also important when the writer wants to focus attention on the object of the verb's action.

Although many composition books warn people against excessive use of the passive, writers should not avoid it completely. Instead its use should be applied wisely. Even in writing about movement, the passive has its place:

The ball *was caught* as Slugger slid home.

If instead, the writer said:

Lefty caught the ball as Slugger slid home.

the attention would be shifted to Lefty. That is not what the writer intended to do.

Interrogative Sentences

An interrogative sentence is a sentence that asks a question. A spoken question is generally signaled by a raised tone at the end of the sentence. A written question is signaled by a *question mark* at the end of the sentence.

There are a limited number of words that can begin a question. Some questions begin with auxiliary verbs such as *is, do, are, can, may, have,* or *has.* The auxiliary comes before the subject. Often this means splitting the verb, with the auxiliary before and the rest of the verb after the subject.

auxiliary	subject	remaining verb
Did	he	*give* her the book?
Will	John	*go* home?
Is	she	*singing* tonight?
Has	the mail	*arrived?*
Were	the dogs	*barking?*
May	Jason	*visit* us?

Occasionally *have* or *is* may be used without a second verb to form a question. The verb comes before the subject in these sentences.

Are they at home?
Is she a singer?
Have you any wool?
Has he a home?

Questions may also begin with one of a small group of words that are used to begin questions: *who, what, where, when, how, why, which, whose.*

Who is coming to dinner?   *How* did they learn of it?
What did he do?   *Why* hasn't John written?
Where are my socks?   *Which* house is yours?
When will you leave?   *Whose* mess is that?

A question may be a single word. One-word questions begin with capitals. When a single word does form the entire question, a previous question or statement is understood.

(Somebody told the secret.)	Who?
(Will he announce the winner?)	When?
(I discovered the treasure.)	How? Where?
(He is not going.)	Why?

Occasionally a question may be phrased in the word order that normally is reserved for declarative sentences. Such questions end with a question mark in written matter. Questions in this form often indicate surprise.

He went to the ball game?
They have been invited to dinner?
She discovered the treasure?

Indirect Questions

Indirect questions are not interrogative sentences. They are declarative sentences and they end in periods. An indirect question is a sentence that mentions or suggests a question. To understand the difference, look below.

Direct

Where do they live?
How much does it cost?
Where did he find it?

Indirect

Ask them where they live.

Find out how much it costs.

She wondered where he found it.

An indirect question should not be worded the same way as a direct question. For example, "Ask them where do they live" is not good wording for an indirect question.

Exclamations

Exclamations are punctuated with exclamation points. An exclamation may express surprise, anger, or other strong emotion. Some words—interjections—are used chiefly in exclamations.

Wow!	Stop!
Phooey!	You rat!
You did it!	How good you are!
Don't hit me!	What a change!

Note that exclamations need not have subjects and verbs. The word order may be the same as or different from that of a declarative sentence.

Commands

Commands are always addressed to "you." In a command the word "you" is generally left out. It is usually understood without being said. A command is considered a full sentence even though the subject ("you") is not indicated.

Bring me the book.	Tell me a story.
Go to sleep.	Count to ten.

Sentence Fragments

Sentence fragments are groups of words that *do not make a grammatical sentence*. Often they do not have a subject and a verb. They are incomplete.

There are many acceptable uses for sentence fragments. Sentence fragments are acceptable as exclamations:

What fun!

How lovely!

Sentence fragments are acceptable as questions, provided that a previous statement or question establishes the nature of the question:

Statement	Fragment
"Mr. Smith is away on vacation."	"For how long?"
"He will be back soon."	"When?"

Sentence fragments are also acceptable as answers to questions.

Question	Fragment Answer
Where did he go?	Upstairs to his room.
Do you like him?	No.
When will he return?	Next week.

Many good writers may use sentence fragments effectively to accomplish a purpose, to establish a certain pace, or to suggest a disjointed quality.

Into the alley he went. Up the fire escape. Over the wall. Around a corner. Into a bar.

Except for the first sentence, the passage above contains only sentence fragments. Such a passage may or may not work well in a given context.

The chief danger of using sentence fragments lies in not knowing that they are fragments, but thinking they are sentences. The writer of the following passage may or may not have known that the last two "sentences" are fragments:

Strolling the ancient city's streets, I seemed to hear the ghosts of history telling of its founding centuries ago. *Of its trade with the Scythians and with tribes up and down the Danube. Telling of Alexander the Great.*

Why is neither a sentence? Let us examine them:

Of its trade with the Scythians, and with the tribes up and down the Danube.

The sentence has no verb. None of the nouns (trade, Scythians, tribes, or Danube) is the subject of the sentence. All are objects of prepositions.

Telling of Alexander the Great.

The only suggestion of a verb is *telling*—the present participle of *tell*. And the only noun is *Alexander the Great*, and that is not the subject of the sentence.

How could this paragraph be corrected to turn all the fragments into sentences? There are several ways.

The entire paragraph can be rewritten as one sentence.

Strolling the ancient city's streets, I seemed to hear the ghosts of history telling of its founding centuries ago, of its trade with the Scythians and with tribes up and down the Danube, and also of Alexander the Great.

Or it can be rewritten by adding a subject to the two fragment sentences.

Strolling the ancient city's streets, I seemed to hear the ghosts of history telling of its founding centuries ago. The ghosts seemed to tell of trade with the Scythians and with tribes up and down the Danube. The ghosts also told of Alexander the Great.

Sentence fragments may be long or short. But unless they are recognized, they cannot be avoided when avoidance is desired. People who are just beginning to master the elements of grammar and composition should try to avoid sentence fragments.

SENTENCE STRUCTURE AND PATTERNS

Most of the sentences examined so far were fairly simple in structure. Each had a subject and verb. Some had a direct object and an indirect object. The subject, verb, or object may have been modified. But in each example there was generally only one subject, one verb, and one of each kind of object. It was fairly easy to identify the subject, verb, and objects in each.

Sentences can grow far more complicated than the examples we have seen. A sentence may have several subjects, verbs, or objects. Some sentences may have

many *phrases* and *clauses*. The more complicated a
sentence becomes, the more difficult it may be to identify the subject and predicate.

Coordinate Elements

One of the simplest ways to enlarge a simple sentence
is to use more than one subject, verb, or object. When
there are multiple elements, it is important to keep
them parallel in form. The multiple elements may be
subjects.

Multiple Subjects

subjects —

Dogs and cats run wild in the street.

Men and women played tennis.

Wisdom and learning are not the same.

Sheep, horses, and pigs live on the farm.

Avoid such ill-matched combinations as "Wisdom,
learning, and to know are not the same." "To know"
is an infinitive and does not fit the pattern established
by "wisdom, learning . . .". "Wisdom, learning, and
knowledge . . ." would be better.

The multiple subject may be a series of phrases instead of individual words.

—————————— subjects ——————————
Going to school, keeping house, and *maintaining a*

job complicate her life.

—————————— subjects ——————————
Antique   tapestries   from   France,   handwoven

Navaho blankets, and *Early American samplers* cover the walls.

There should be no comma between the last subject and the verb. And, of course, the verb must agree with the subject.

Sometimes one preposition will work for all elements of a series: Dreams *of* wealth, fame, and happiness kept her going.

It is acceptable either to repeat the preposition or to allow the one preposition to govern the various elements: Dreams *of* wealth, *of* fame, and *of* happiness kept her going. (Wealth, fame, and happiness are all understood to be objects of the preposition "of.") It is not good style to repeat it once and not again. For example, "Dreams of wealth, fame, and of happiness kept her going."

The same preposition may not work for all the elements in a series. It is then necessary to give the appropriate preposition for each element.

The multiple elements may be verbs:

Multiple Verbs

verbs

He *cut, fit,* and *sewed* the clothes in one day.

verbs

She *tried, failed,* and *tried* again.

verbs

The children *dried* their tears and *began* to sing.

Note that two or more verbs may accompany a single subject. Sometimes the verbs are simple. Sometimes, as in the third example, the entire predicate may be multiple.

It is possible to have more than one verb, each with its objects or modifiers. A comma should not separate the subject from either verb.

We *ate* our sandwiches and *drank* our milk.

Jimmy *waved* good-by to his friends and *drove* home slowly.

When using auxiliaries with verbs, it is important to make sure that the tenses are maintained correctly. It is easy to forget that the auxiliary verb governs all the verbs in the series.

He has *come* and *gone*. "Gone" is correct, not "went" because "has" governs both past participles.

The time machine *has not been*, perhaps never *will be*, invented.

Two different auxiliaries are needed: "has been" for the present perfect tense and "will be" for the future. The past participle goes with both.

The multiple elements may be objects:

Multiple Objects

Direct

We ate *fish* and *chips*.
└─ objects ─┘

Felicia bought *books, clothes,* and *records*.
└────── objects ──────┘

I enjoy *going to movies, riding a bicycle,* and *building birdhouses*.
└──────────── objects ────────────┘

115

Indirect

$$\overbrace{\hspace{3cm}}^{\text{indirect objects}}$$

Give the tickets to *Tom*, *Dick*, and *Harry*.

$$\overbrace{\hspace{3cm}}^{\text{indirect objects}}$$

Did you throw the ball to *him* or at *him?*

In all the examples given so far there has been either one subject and several verbs, one verb and several subjects, or one verb and several objects. The verbs, the subjects and the objects may be multiple.

$$\overbrace{}^{\text{two subjects}} \quad \overbrace{}^{\text{two verbs}}$$

a. *Dick* and *Jane ran* and *skipped* all the way.

Note that both subjects govern both verbs.

$$\overbrace{}^{\text{two subjects}} \quad \overbrace{}^{\text{two verbs}}$$

b. The *cat* and the *kitten sniffed* and *ate* the

$$\overbrace{}^{\text{two direct objects}}$$

fish and *chicken.*

Both subjects may govern both verbs, *and* both verbs may govern both objects.

$$\overbrace{}^{\text{two subjects}} \ \overbrace{}^{\text{1st verb}} \ \overbrace{}^{\text{1st object}} \ \overbrace{}^{\text{2nd verb}}$$

c. The *cat* and the *kitten ate* the *fish* and *drank* the

$$\overbrace{}^{\text{2nd object}}$$

milk.

Example **c** differs from example **b**. In **c**, both subjects govern both verbs. But each verb has its own direct object.

Clauses

A clause is a group of words that has a subject and predicate. A clause may be *independent* or it may be *subordinate*.

An *independent clause* can be a sentence in itself. It can also be the main clause of a larger sentence. The main clause is sometimes called the "basic sentence."

A *subordinate clause* has a subject and a predicate, too. But it cannot stand by itself as a complete sentence. It depends on the main clause. The subordinate clause is sometimes called a "dependent clause."

subordinate clause ⸌‾‾⸍   ⸌‾‾‾‾‾‾‾‾‾‾‾‾⸍ independent clause
If it rains, we'll go home.

"We'll go home" can be a separate sentence. It is an independent clause.

"If it rains" cannot stand alone as a separate sentence. It is a subordinate clause.

Compound Sentences

Compound sentences are made up of two or more *coordinate* independent clauses. *Coordinate* in this sense means of equal importance. A compound sentence is made up of clauses that could each be separate sentences if the writer wanted to write them as separate sentences.

We tried and we failed.

I tried to buy sugar, but the store was out of it.

He will pick up the package tomorrow, or you will have to mail it.

We climbed up the trail, and the snow nearly trapped us.

John didn't win the trophy; he didn't even try.

Henry will prepare the dessert, Molly will make the salad, and I'll cook the main course.

People are born, people die, but the earth spins on.

Notice that the last two examples have more than two independent clauses. They are said to be in series.

A series of three or more independent clauses may eliminate the coordinating conjunction after the comma in all but the last of the series.

Each of the above sentences can be rewritten as two or more separate sentences.

We tried. And we failed.

I tried to buy sugar. But the store was out of it.

He will pick up the package tomorrow. Or you will have to mail it.

We climbed up the trail. And the snow nearly trapped us.

John didn't win the trophy. He didn't even try.

Henry will prepare the dessert. Molly will make the salad. And I'll cook the main course.

People are born. People die. But the earth spins on.

The independent clauses of a compound sentence may be separated by:

- a comma and a coordinate conjunction (*and, and so, but, or, nor, for, yet, so*): *I tried to buy sugar, but the store was out of it.*
- a semicolon if there is no coordinate conjunction: *John didn't win the trophy; he didn't even try.*
- a coordinating conjunction alone only if the two clauses are very short: *We tried and we failed.*
- a comma may replace a semicolon only in very short sentences: *Sometimes you win, sometimes you lose.*

The subjects of the independent clauses in a sentence may be identical, or they may be different. But the subject must be stated in each clause. If it is not, the sentence is not a compound sentence.

Notice the difference between these sentences.

He ran, and he jumped.

He ran and jumped.

The first sentence is a compound sentence. It can be separated into two sentences: *He ran. And he jumped.* The second sentence is not a compound sentence. Its subject is stated only once, and it is a simple sentence with coordinate verbs.

It is important to recognize the difference between the two kinds of sentences. The second sentence should not have a comma before "and." The first sentence should have a comma before "and."

Because independent clauses can be combined into a single sentence, some people have a tendency to overdo the combining or to punctuate incorrectly. Some common errors that arise from this tendency are:

Run-on Sentences

Run-on sentences are sentences in which too many independent clauses have been combined. They are difficult to read. Run-on sentences can usually be corrected by separating the clauses into individual sentences. The conjunctions that connect the clauses of run-on sentences can then be eliminated.

Run-on Sentence

The wicked witch cast a spell *so* the prince fell asleep, *and* the princess didn't know what to do, *but* the king sent the knight to fight the dragon, *then* the prince awoke.

Corrected Sentence
The wicked witch cast a spell. The prince fell asleep, and the princess didn't know what to do. The king sent the knight to fight the dragon. Then the prince awoke.

Comma Splice

A comma splice occurs when a comma without a coordinating conjunction separates the main clauses of a compound sentence. A comma splice can easily be repaired in one of four ways.

- insert a coordinating conjunction
- replace the comma with a semicolon
- rewrite the clauses to make separate sentences
- turn one clause into a subordinate clause

Comma Splice
The moon hid behind a cloud, all the world turned dark.

Correction
The moon hid behind a cloud, and all the world turned dark.
or
The moon hid behind a cloud; all the world turned dark.
or
The moon hid behind a cloud. All the world turned dark.

or

Because the moon hid behind a cloud, all the world turned dark.

Fused Sentences

Fused sentences are two or more sentences joined without punctuation. Often the writer is under the mistaken notion that a compound sentence has been created. Fused sentences can be separated into individual sentences.

Fused Sentence
He didn't ask me he just did it.

Corrected Sentence
He didn't ask me. He just did it.

Fused Sentence
John said he was going to enter the big race then his mother said that she would not allow it.

Corrected Sentence
John said he was going to enter the big race. Then his mother said that she would not allow it.

Complex Sentences

A complex sentence has an independent clause and a subordinate clause. The subordinate clause is usually introduced by a subordinate conjunction (*if, because, although, when, as soon as, whenever, even though, before, since, unless, until,* etc.).

The subordinate clause may come before or after the main clause. When it comes before the main clause, a comma usually separates the clauses.

I'll go to the dance *if mother lets me.* [subordinate clause]

If mother lets me, I'll go to the dance. [subordinate clause]

Because I laughed, the teacher asked me to leave the room. [subordinate clause]

The teacher asked me to leave the room *because I laughed.* [subordinate clause]

When the rains fall, the river overflows. [subordinate clause]

He will return *as soon as he has train fare.* [subordinate clause]

Do you know the man *who sat next to you?* [subordinate clause]

We enjoyed the party *that you gave.* [subordinate clause]

Because the subordinate clause of a complex sentence has a subject and a verb, some people make the mistake of trying to set it up as a separate sentence. This results in sentence fragments. In this case, these sentence fragments can be corrected in two ways.

- The fragment can be woven into the main sentence.
- The subordinating conjunction can be eliminated, and the subordinate clause can become a main clause.

Fragment

He left the scene very quickly. Because the police were pursuing him for the theft.

122

Correction

He left the scene very quickly because the police were pursuing him for the theft.

or

He left the scene very quickly. The police were pursuing him for the theft.

Compound-complex Sentences

Compound-complex sentences are sentences that have two or more independent clauses and at least one subordinate clause.

┌── subordinate clause ──┐ ┌──── independent clause ────┐
After the war ended, prices continued to rise, and
┌── independent clause ──┐
the black market thrived.

┌── independent clause ──┐ ┌── independent clause ──┐
Everybody stopped speaking, and the ticking clock
┌──────────────────────┐ ┌── subordinate clause ──
was all that could be heard when the maharishi took
the stage.

┌────── independent clause ──────┐ ┌── subordinate ──
The children filed out of the school as soon as the
──clause─┐ ┌──────── independent clause ────────┐
bell rang, and the janitors checked the classrooms
┌──── subordinate clause ────┐
because they wanted to clean them.

Subordinate Clauses as Subjects, Objects, Modifiers

When subordinate clauses occur in sentences, they often fill the job of a particular part of speech. The entire clause may serve as a noun, an adjective, or an adverb.

When a subordinate clause fills the role of a noun, it may serve as a subject or an object.

Subject

How the pyramids were built remains a mystery.
<small>└── subject ──┘</small>

That she is an impostor cannot be proven.
<small>└── subject ──┘</small>

What he found out is a secret.
<small>└── subject ──┘</small>

Object of a Verb

The architect discovered *how the pyramids were built*.
<small>└── object ──┘</small>

Can you prove *that she is an impostor?*
<small>└── object ──┘</small>

We know *that he found the secret.*
<small>└── object ──┘</small>

Object of a Preposition

John learned about *what had been said.*
<small>└── object ──┘</small>

She will go to *whatever school she chooses.*
<small>└── object ──┘</small>

Predicate Nominative

The story is *that he disappeared.*
<small>└─ predicate nominative ─┘</small>

It seems *that he did run away.*
<small>└─ predicate nominative ─┘</small>

When a subordinate clause fills the role of an adverb, it modifies a verb, adjective, or another adverb.

Modifying a Verb

He will *return* *as soon as he has train fare.*
<small>verb └── subordinate clause ──┘</small>

Sally will *dance* *if you ask her.*
<small>verb └── subordinate clause ──┘</small>

124

Modifying an Adjective

adjective **subordinate clause**

The movie was funnier *than I expected.*

adjective **subordinate clause**

Simon is as tall *as I am.*

Modifying an Adverb

adverb

She ran quickly *as a gazelle might.*

adverb

He gossiped more indiscreetly *than I imagined possible.*

When a subordinate clause fills the role of an adjective, it generally modifies a noun.

Modifying a Noun

noun

I like the dress *that you bought.*

noun

I find myself on the street *where you live.*

noun

The man *who is wise* avoids trouble.

To summarize: A *noun clause* is a clause that functions as a noun in a sentence. An *adverbial clause* functions as an adverb in a sentence. An *adjectival clause* functions as an adjective in a sentence.

A noun clause *is not* a clause that begins with a noun. An adverbial clause *is not* a clause that begins with an adverb. An adjectival clause *is not* a clause that begins with an adjective.

Each of the clauses is so labeled because of its function in a sentence.

Periodic Sentences

A periodic sentence is one in which the main clause

comes at the end. Two or more clauses or phrases—often parallel in construction—lead up to the main clause. A periodic sentence can be very dramatic in effect if it is used well and infrequently. In a periodic sentence, it is important that the main clause justify the lead-up.

Periodic Sentence with Subordinate Clauses
Because he had burned their villages, because he had ignored their pleas for mercy, because his

⌐— main clause —

cruelty increased with his successes, *they attacked*

⌐
him with unexpected savagery.

Periodic Sentence with Phrases
In winter, in summer, in good times and bad, in

⌐—————— main clause ——————⌐

health and sickness, *he always had time for others*.

Working long hours, saving every penny she could,

denying herself luxuries, using every resource she

⌐——————————— main clause ———————————⌐

had, *she managed to save enough for an education*.

By the light of the moon, in out-of-the-way places,

⌐—— main clause ——⌐

unseen by mortals, *the wee folk gather*.

Phrases and Verb Forms

A phrase is a group of words that together have some meaning. A phrase does not have to have a subject and a verb, but it may. A clause or a short sentence may be called a phrase, but most phrases would not be called clauses. Clauses must have subjects and verbs.

Phrases may be used to modify nouns, adjectives, verbs, and even complete sentences. The phrases may be used in the same way that single words may be used in a sentence.

Apposition

A noun or pronoun may have a noun or a phrase in *apposition*. That is, a noun or phrase may stand next to the noun or pronoun and extend its meaning.

Miss Grimsby, *our teacher,* is very strict.

We, *the committee,* are responsible for the decision.

My sister *Rosalie* has red hair.

You, *the organizer of the event,* deserve our thanks.

The girl *over there* is shy.

The book *under the counter* is rare.

The man *drinking coffee* is the spy.

We thanked our teacher, *Miss Grimsby.*

He winked at my sister *Rosalie.*

Notice that either the subject or the object may have a word or phrase in apposition. It is the first noun or pronoun—not the one in apposition—that determines the form of the verb. (We, the committee, *are,* not *is;* You—deserve, not "the organizer . . . deserves," etc.)

Object Complement

Some verbs seem to have two objects. The second object is not really in apposition to the first. The second is an *object complement.*

The council elected John *president*.

We appointed Sara *leader*.

They named him *king of the jungle*.

An adjective can also be an object complement.

The heat made the plant *brown*.

Opposition turned the deal *sour*.

Verb Forms in Noun Positions

The subject of a sentence need not be a noun. It may be a clause. It may also be an infinitive of a verb.

To travel requires money.

To speak honestly is difficult.

Even though the infinitive *(to speak)* may take the place of a noun, its verbal nature is maintained. It is modified by an adverb *(honestly)* as a verb would be modified. A noun would be modified by an adjective.

The infinitive can also serve as an object.

He likes *to sit*.

He wants *to play* hockey.

The object *(to play)* is still basically a verb. It has its own object *(hockey)*.

A *gerund* is the *-ing* form of a verb when used as a noun while conveying the meaning of a verb. A gerund may serve as a subject or an object. Many gerunds have become nouns in their own right.

Traveling requires money.

His *going* relieves us of a problem.

We enjoy *singing*.

Good *singing* gives us pleasure.

Singing well gives us pleasure.

Note that a gerund *(singing)* may be modified by an adjective *(good)* or an adverb *(well)*. When the gerund has more of a noun sense, an adjective modifies it; when it has more of a verbal sense, an adverb modifies it.

Gerunds have more nounlike functions than infinitives. Gerunds may be used in apposition, as object complements, and as objects of prepositions.

Participles and Other Modifiers

A modifier may modify a word, a phrase, a clause, or a whole sentence. A modifier may be a word, a phrase, a clause, or a whole sentence.

As you know, a clause or a phrase may function as an adjective, an adverb, or a noun. The phrase or clause that modifies must be placed in the correct relationship to the word it modifies.

Having seen the house, she left.
Though sick, he went to work.

These examples are grammatically acceptable. The sentences could also be rewritten.

She left *having seen the house.*
He went to work *though sick.*

They still make sense. That is because the modifying phrase logically belongs with the pronouns *(she* and *he).*

Dangling Modifiers

These occur when a modifier does not modify the subject of the main clause. Dangling modifiers usually occur at the beginnings of sentences.

Sentences have to be rewritten to correct the dangling modifier.

Dangling Modifier
Though sick, I saw him at work.

Correction
Though he was sick, I saw him at work.

Dangling Modifier
After running the race, we saw him faint.

Correction
We saw him faint after running the race.

Notice that the problem with the dangling modifier occurs because it has no subject of its own. The subject of the main clause is usually taken to be the subject of the modifier. That creates some ridiculous images. Once a writer learns to recognize the silliness of what was said unintentionally, that writer will make fewer and fewer such errors.

┌─ dangling modifier ─┐
On returning home, the door slammed shut.
(The door was not returning home.)
┌─ dangling modifier ─┐
Falling from the tree, the girl caught the apple.
(In this case, the apple was falling from the tree, not the girl.)

Absolute Construction

To complicate matters, there are some modifiers that

130

modify the whole sentence. This kind of modifier is said to be an absolute construction.

┌─── absolute construction ───┐
The moment having arrived, we went inside the church. ┌─ absolute construction ─┐

┌─ absolute construction ─┐
The cause lost, we abandoned our headquarters.

┌ absolute construction ┐
┌──────────┐
Apparently, the city was blacked out.

Such clauses, phrases, and individual words are acceptable English. They should not be confused with dangling modifiers. Sentence modifiers modify the whole sentence. Dangling modifiers unintentionally modify the wrong elements in a sentence.

Parenthetical Remarks

Occasionally a writer wants to insert a comment or explanation within a sentence. That comment or explanation may not be a part of the actual sentence construction. The insertions are known as *parenthetical remarks.*

There are several kinds of parenthetical remarks and several different ways of punctuating them: with commas; with parentheses; with brackets; with dashes.

Commas are used only when the parenthetical remark is very short and flows well within the sentence.

My friend, *the one who moved to Chicago,* just got married.

John, *old and infirm though he is,* walked all the way home.

Commas are used in these sentences only for *nonrestrictive* phrases or clauses.

Nonrestrictive

My son, *the doctor,* sent me a letter.

(The writer has one son who happens to be a doctor.)

Restrictive

My son *the doctor* sent me a letter.

(The writer has more than one son. The one who is a doctor sent her the letter.)

Parentheses are used for longer material, further explanation, and side comments.

The whole group (except for those who had resigned) agreed to settle the debt.

The warriors had not really left town (as their letter seemed to indicate) but were waiting in ambush.

The article on cryogenics (see page 38) suggests that the future may hold great appeal for some sufferers

He said he woodn't (*sic*) go. (*Sic* means that t word was originally written that way.)

Note that parentheses may be used for whole sentences as well as words or phrases.

Brackets are usually reserved for more formal situations than parentheses. But they may be used also in place of parentheses.

. . . life, liberty, and the *pursuit* [italics added] o happiness.

The women live in purdah [veils as required by religion and custom] and few men ever see their faces.

Dashes are used in the same way as parentheses are, to set off a parenthetical remark.

The medium spoke of spirits—poltergeists, ghosts, ghouls—as if she thought we all believed in them.

A two-week camping trip—whenever the weather allows us to leave—is the high point of our planned vacation.

Whether a writer uses parentheses, brackets, or dashes is often a matter of personal choice. Some writers tend to use parentheses; others use dashes. The important point is to be sure that the sentence that goes around the parenthetical remark makes sense in its own right. If you remove the parenthetical remark, the sentence should be grammatically correct.

SENTENCES INTO PARAGRAPHS

Almost everything we write—letters, essays, stories, memoranda, term papers—is divided into paragraphs. Why do we make the divisions? How do we know what goes into a paragraph and when to stop and begin the next one?

A paragraph is a unit of thought. A writer tries to organize each paragraph around one theme or idea, and groups sentences that deal with each theme in one paragraph. Then the next theme is explored in the next paragraph. The theme may be highly structured with a main idea and subdivisions of that main idea. Or the theme may be loose enough so that the only organizing theme is the writer's perception of connected thoughts.

Often a theme is stated in the paragraph's topic sentence. The remaining sentences in the paragraph expand on the topic sentence by giving specifics. Often, but not always, the topic sentence is the first sentence of the paragraph.

Within a paragraph, the ideas should move easily from one sentence to the next. There should be a logic in the progression from sentence to sentence. The logic should be clear to the reader as well as to the writer.

What is true for each paragraph is also true for groups of paragraphs. There should be a clear logic in the progression from paragraph to paragraph. Often the progression of ideas can be seen just by reading the topic sentences in each paragraph.

These are some general rules for developing paragraphs:

1. Each paragraph should present a *unit*. It must be a grouping of sentences that are related to each other and to the main thought.

2. Each paragraph should present a complete thought and expand on it fully before ending the paragraph and beginning the next.

3. Within the paragraph, there should be a logic of movement: from general statement to specifics; from specific statements to general ones; from the beginning of an action to the end of the action; from a statement to a refutation to a re-examination of

the original statement. The possibilities are numerous.

4. There should be a good balance of kinds of sentences. At times it is very effective to repeat the same structure in sentence after sentence within a paragraph. But this stylistic device can be overused. It is more effective to vary the rhythm, length, and construction of sentences.

5. It is important to maintain the same person throughout a paragraph. Switching from "you" to "one" to "they" can be very disconcerting to a reader.

6. It is important to maintain the same tense for the same subject within a paragraph. Events in the past should not be described in the present and also in the past. At times, some of the events in a paragraph may have taken place in the far past, others over a period of time. The sequence of tenses should make the time relationship clear.

7. The introduction of a new topic requires the beginning of a new paragraph.

Some paragraphs require special attention. They have special places within a written work and serve special functions.

The Opening Paragraph

The opening paragraph is the first paragraph of a written work. A major function of the opening paragraph is to engage the reader's attention. There are several customary ways of doing this.

1. Ask a question. The question should go to the heart of the material you deal with. The question may be asked as a direct question ("Are sharks monogamous?") or as in indirect question ("We wanted to know if sharks are monogamous").
2. Make a statement. The statement should be clearly worded. No qualifying phrases should offset the force of the statement. The statement may be the basic theme of the work or it may be the reason for writing the work ("There is no good published material on the breeding life of the shark").
3. Begin with a quotation. You may then proceed to agree or disagree with the quotation. In either case, the quotation should be directly related to the theme of the work.
4. Present a short anecdote. The anecdote may be directly or obliquely related to the rest of the piece.
5. Cite an opinion by an authority, or offer a common view with which you agree or disagree.

Transitional Paragraphs

In a sense, every paragraph makes a transition from the paragraph before to the paragraph after. Some paragraphs, however, must make a major transition from one block of ideas to another block of ideas.

There are several devices that make transitions flow more smoothly.

1. Summarize what has gone before, and lead in to the next theme with a transitional word or phrase such as "on the other hand," "but," "however," etc.
2. Find a link for the ideas before and the ideas after, and lead from one to the other.
3. Use a short paragraph that picks up a word or phrase from the preceding paragraph. Then introduce a main idea for what will follow.

Concluding Paragraphs

A concluding paragraph is the finishing touch to a piece of writing. When a reader encounters a good concluding paragraph, there is no temptation to turn the page to see what comes next. How is this accomplished?

1. By summarizing the ideas that have gone before. This technique is effective only with long pieces of writing.
2. By drawing conclusions about what has been said.
3. By stating further questions to be explored at another time.

PICKING A PREPOSITION

The following list contains forms of verbs, adjectives, and nouns that regularly appear in combination with certain prepositions. Following each entry word are the prepositions which are idiomatically linked with that word.

Picking the right preposition is often a matter of idiom. Related verbs such as *acquiesce, agree,* and *concur* might be thought to agree in every detail in the choice of prepositions, but they do not. So consulting a list of idiomatic expressions is the only sure method of avoiding error. Even people who work with the language every day—such as professional writers and speakers—often consult such a list. The list is not intended to imply that the entry word must be followed or preceded by a preposition, but rather that in certain contexts it is often used with that preposition. Only usages that commonly give difficulty are treated.

The prepositions listed are the ones most often used with the words in question; where the choice is determined by a particular sense of the entry word, the sense is indicated and illustrated when an example of the particular combination is not likely to come to the reader's mind readily. No adverbial usage is included, nor are the countless combinations of entry words followed by infinitives. Phrasal verbs, such as *bottom out* and *carry forward,* are also omitted.

abashed at

abhorrence of

abhorrent to

ability at or with
    (at mechanics; with tools)
abound in or with

absolve of or *from*

accede to

access to

accessible to

accession of or *to*
  (*of property; to the throne*)

acclimate or *acclimatize to*

accommodate to or *with*
  (*to changing circumstances; with
  everything she requested*)

accompanied by or *with*
  (*by her husband; with every
  difficulty imaginable*)

accord (n.) *between, of,* or *with;*
  (v.) *to* or *with* (*accord every consideration to her; a statement that
  accords with the law*)

account (v.) *for* or *to*
  (*for things; to persons*)

accrue to

acquiesce in

acquit of

adapt for, from, or *to*

addicted to (plus noun, but not plus
  infinitive): *addicted to heroin; to
  taking heroin; not to take heroin*

adept at or *in*

adequate for or *to* (*for a goal or purpose; to a need*)

adjacent to

admit to, into, or *of* (*admit one to or
  into a club; a passage admitting to
  the lobby; a matter that admits of
  several views*)

adverse to

advocate (n.) *of;* (v.) *for*

affiliate (v.) *with* or *to*

affinity of, between, or *with*

akin to

alien (adj.) *to* or *from*

ally (v.) *to* or *with*

aloof from

amenable to

amused by or *at*

analogous in, to, or *with* (in qual-
  ities; *to* or *with each other*)

analogy of, between, to or *with*

angry at, with, or *about*

antidote to, for, or *against*

antipathy to, toward, or *against*

anxious for or *about*

apprehensive or *or for*
  (*of danger; for one's welfare*)

apprise of

apropos of

arrogate to or *for*

aspiration toward or *after*

aspire to, toward, or *after*

assent to

attempt (n.) *at* or *on* (*at realizing an
  achievement; on a person's life*)

attended by or *with* (*by persons; by
  or with conditions or circumstances*)

attest to

attune to

augment by or *with*

averse to

aversion for, to, or *toward*

basis for, in, or *of* (*for a rumor;
  in fact* or *in law; of a medicinal
  compound; of* or *for an official's
  authority*)

bid (v.) *for* or *on*
  (*for nomination; on property*)

blame (v.) *for* or *on* (*blame her for
  the delay; blame the delay on him*)

blink (v.) *at* (sense of *connive;* without preposition, sense of *ignore* or
  overlook)

boast (n., v.) *of* or *about*

boggle at

capacity of or *for* (*of four quarts for
  growth*)

capitalize at or *on* (at $4 million; on an opponent's mistakes)

careless about, in, or *of* (about her attendance; in her speech; of or about the children's welfare)

caution (v.) *about* or *against*

center (v.) *on, upon, in* or *at* (but not *around*)

charge (v.) *for* or *with* (for services; with manslaughter; with a duty; with strong emotion)

clear (adj.) *of;* (v.) *of* or *from*

climb up (though usually redundant), *down*

coincide with

common (adj.) *to*

comparable to or *with*

compare with or *to* (like things that are strictly comparable, *with* each other; unlike things *to* each other in sense of *liken;* things *with* each other in sense of *be worthy of comparison*)

compatible with

complementary to

compliment (n., v.) *on*

concern (n., v.) *about, in,* or *with*

concur in or *with* (in a plan or policy; with a person or view)

conducive to

confide in or *to*

conform or *conformity to* or *with*

connive at or *with* (at a fraud; with an accomplice)

consequent (adj.) or *consequential to, on,* or *upon*

consist of or *in* (an alloy consisting chiefly of nickel; treason, which consists in aiding the enemies of one's country)

consistent with

contemporary with

contemporary with

contemptuous of

contend with, against, about, or *over* (with or against rivals, enemies, or unfavorable circumstances; about or over disputed matters)

contiguous to

contingent on or *upon*

contrast (n.) *between, to,* or *with* (between things; in contrast to or with); (v.) *with*

conversant with

convict (v.) *of*

correspond to or *with* (a statement not corresponding to or with his earlier account; a part that corresponds to the bore of a musket; when I corresponded with her)

culminate in

cure (v.) *of*

decide on, upon, for, or *against* (on or upon a matter or issue; for or against a principal in a legal action)

deficient in

deprive of

derive from

desire (n.) *for*

desirous of

desist from

despair (v.) *of*

destined for (for an end, use, or purpose; for a locality)

destitute of

destructive to or *of*

deviate (v.) *from*

devoid of

devolve from, on, to or *upon*

differ from, on, over, or *with* (from another person in outlook; on or over issues; with a second party to an argument) *different from* or *than (a job different from his; an outcome different from what we expected; how different things seem now than yesterday). Different from* is the preferred form when it works readily—when *from* is followed by a single word or short clause. *Different than* is most acceptable when it aids conciseness—when *from* could not be used except ponderously and when *than* is followed by a condensed clause.

differentiate between, among, or *from*

diminution of

disappointed by, in, or *with (by or in a person; in or with a thing)*

discourage from

disdain (n.) *for*

disengage from

disgusted with, at or *by (with a person* or *an action; at an action or behavior; by a personal quality, action,* or *behavior)*

dislike of

dispossess of or *from*

disqualify for or *from*

dissent (n., v.) *from*

dissimilar to

dissociate from

dissuade from

distaste for

distinguish from, between, or *among (distinguish one species from another; distinguish between* or *among shades of meaning)*

distrustful of

divest of

dote on

emanate from

embellish with

emigrate from

empty (adj.) *of*

enamored of or *with*

encroach on or *upon*

end (v.) *with* or *in (with a light dessert* or *with a benediction; in divorce)*

endow with

entrust to or *with (entrust a mission to a confidant; entrust a friend with a mission)*

envelop in

envious of

essential (adj.) *to* or *for;* (n.) *of*

estrange from

exclusive of

excuse (v.) *for* or *from (for a fault; from an obligation* or *duty)*

exonerate of or *from*

expect from or *of (expect an apology from a mistaken person; expect integrity of a partner)*

experience (n.) *in* or *of*

expert (adj., n.) *in, at,* or *with (in or at weaving; with a loom)*

expressive of

exude from

favorable to, toward, or *for*

fear (n.) *of* or *for (of death; for my safety)*

fond of

fondness for

foreign to

free (adj., v.) *of* or *from*

freedom of or *from*

friend of or *to*

frightened of or *by*

fugitive (n., adj.) *from*

grateful to or *for (to a person; for a benefit)*

grieve for, after, or *at*

habitual with

hanker after

heal by or *of*

hinder from

hindrance to

hint (v.) *at*

honor (v.) *by, for,* or *with* (*by* or *with a citation for bravery; for his bravery; with one's presence*)

hope (n.) *for* or *of;* (v.) *for*

identical with or *to*

identify (oneself) *with* (*with the hero of a play*)

immigrate to

impatient at or *with* (*at a condition of affairs; with a person*)

impervious to

implicit in

impressed by or *with*

improve on or *upon*

inaccessible to

incentive (n.) *to* or *for*

incidental to

incongruous to

inconsistent with

incorporate in, into, or *with*

independent (adj.) *of*

infer from

inferior to

infested with

influence (n.) *on, upon, over,* or *of*

infuse with

inimical to or *toward*

initiate into

innocent of

inquire about, after, or *into*

inroad into

insight into

inspire by or *with*

instruct in

intention of

intercede with, for, or *(on behalf of)*

intrude on, upon, into

inundated with

invest in or *with* (*in bonds; with the rank and duties of an office*)

involve in

isolate from

jealous of or *for* (*of his power; for her rights and welfare*)

justified in

lack (v.) *in* (*lacking in support*); or transitive usage (*lack support*)

laden with

lament (n., v.) *for* or *over*

laugh (n.) *at* or *over;* (v.) *at*

level (v.) *at* or *with* (*level a gun or a charge at a person; level wood with a plane; with a person—that is, be honest in dealing*)

liable for or *to* (*for an act; for or to a duty or service; to a superior*)

liken to

martyr (n.) *to;* (v.) *for*

mastery of or *over* (*of a subject; of or over an adversary or obstacle*)

means of, for, or *to*

meddle in or *with*

mediate between or *among*

meditate on or *upon*

militate against or *(rarely) for*

mindful of

mistrustful of

mock at

monopoly of

muse on, upon, or *over*

necessary (adj., n.) *for* or *to*

necessity for, to, or *of*

need (n.) *for* or *of*

neglectful of

negligent in or *of*

oblivious of or *to*

observant of

obtrude on or *upon*

occasion for or *of (for rejoicing; of my visit)*
occupied by or *with*
offend against
opportunity of or *for*
opposite (adj.) to or *from; (n.) of*
opt for or *against*
original (adj.) with
originate in or *with*
overwhelm by or *with*
parallel (adj.) to; (n.) between or *with*
partake in or *of*
patient (adj.) with or *of*
peculiar to
permeate into or *through*
permeated by
permit (v.) of (a rule that permits of two interpretations)
persevere in or *against*
persist in
persuaded by, of, or *into*
pertinent to
pervert (v.) from
possessed of, by, or *with (of great wealth; of a keen wit; by* or *with an urge to kill)*
possibility of or *for*
precedence of or *over*
precedent (adj.) to; (n.) for or *of (for a ruling; of seating members according to rank)*
preclude from
prefer to (prefer concerts to opera)
pregnant by or *with (by a person; with significance)*
prejudicial to
preoccupied by or *with*
preparatory to
prerequisite (adj.) to; (n.) of
preside at or *over*
presume on or *upon*
prevail over, against, on, upon, or

with (over or *against an adversary; on, upon,* or *with a person to provide a service)*
prodigal (adj.) of
productive of
proficient in or *at*
profit (v.) by or *from*
prohibit from
prone to
provide for, against, or *with (for or against an emergency; for a dependent child; for annual elections, by law; with food and medicine)*
pursuant to
qualify for or *as*
receptive to
reconcile to or *with (to hard times; one's belief with another's)*
redolent of
regard (n.) for or *to (for a person; in or with regard to a matter)*
repent of
replete with
respect (n.) for, to, or *of (for a person; with* or *in respect to; in respect of)*
responsibility for
restrain from
revel in
rich in
rob of
satiate with
saturate with
scared at or *by*
secure (adj.) in
similar to
slave (n.) to or *of*
solicitous of, about, or *for*
subject (adj.) to
suffer from
suitable for; to
superior (adj.) to

sympathetic to or toward
sympathy for, toward, or with (for or toward a person or cause; in sympathy with a cause)
tendency to or toward
thrill (v.) to, at, or with (to or at a source of delight; with delight)
tolerance for, toward, or of (for, toward, of persons or causes; of pain; of a scientific instrument)
treat (v.) as, to, of, or with (as a friend; to a meal; of a subject or topic; with another person in negotiations)
vary from

vest (v.) in or with (authority vested in an official; an official vested with authority)
vie with
void (adj.) of
vulnerable to
wait (v.) for or on (for one who was delayed; on a customer or patient)
want (n.) of; (v.) for (did not want for money)
wanting (adj.) in
wary of
yearn for, after or over
zeal for or in

PREFIXES AND SUFFIXES

In today's world of mass communications, big business, and high technology, new words are constantly being formed. Many of these words are old terms to which a combining form has been added. A knowledge, therefore, of the meanings of common prefixes and suffixes is an invaluable aid to anyone dealing with words. The following lists are designed to serve as a handy reference.

Prefixes

a-[1], an-	Without; not; *amoral.*
a-[2]	1. On; in: *abed.*
	2. In the direction of: *astern.*
ab-[1]	Away from: *aboral.*
ab-[2]	Used to indicate a centimeter-gram-second system electromagnetic unit: *abcoulomb.*

ac-, ad-	Toward; to: *admit*.
acro-	1. Height: *acrophobia*.
	2. Tip; beginning: *acronym*.
aero-	1. Air; atmosphere: *aeroballistics*.
	2. Aviation: *aeronautics*.
agro-	Field; soil: *agrology*.
ambi-	Both: *ambidexterity*.
amphi-	1. Both: *amphibiotic*.
	2. Around: *amphitheater*.
ana-	1. Again; anew: *anamnesis*.
	2. Backward; back: *anaplasia*.
ante-	1. Earlier; prior to: *antebellum*.
	2. Before; in front of: *anteroom*.
apo-	Away from: *apogee*.
archaeo-, archeo-	Ancient; primitive: *archaeology*.
archi-, arch-	Chief; highest: *archduke*.
astro-	Star; outer space: *astrodome*.
audio-	1. Hearing: *audition*.
	2. Sound: *audiophile*.
auto-	1. Self; same: *autobiography*.
	2. Automatic: *autopilot*.
bacterio-	Bacteria: *bacteriogenic*.
baro-	Weight; pressure: *barometer*.
bathy-, batho-	Deep; deep-sea: *bathysphere*.
bi-, bin-	Two: *biannual*.
biblio-	Book: *bibliophile*.
bio-	Life; living organisms: *biomass*.
by-	Secondary: *byway*.
calci-	Calcium; calcium salt: *calcification*.
carbo-	Carbon: *carbohydrate*.
cardio-	Heart: *cardiovascular*.
cata-	1. Down: *catapult*.
	2. Reverse; degenerative: *cataplasia*.
centi-	1. One hundredth: *centimeter*.

	2. One hundred: *centipede*.
centro-	Center: *centrosphere*.
cephalo-	Head: *cephalopod*.
cerebro-	Brain; cerebrum: *cerebrovascular*.
chemo-	Chemicals; chemical: *chemotherapy*.
chromato-	Color: *chromatophore*.
chromo-	Color: *chromogen*.
chrono-	Time: *chronometer*.
circum-	Around; about: *circumscribe*.
cis-	On this side: *cisatlantic*.
co-, com-, col-, con-	Together; with: *coeducation*.
contra-	Against; opposite: *contraposition*.
cosmo-	Universe; world: *cosmochemistry*.
counter-	Contrary; opposite; opposing: *counteract*.
cranio-	Skull: *craniotomy*.
cryo-	Cold; freezing: *cryogenics*.
crypto-	Hidden; secret: *cryptogram*.
cyclo-	Circle; cycle: *cyclometer*.
cyto-	Cell: *cytoplasm*.
de-	1. Reverse: *decriminalize*.
	2. Remove; remove from: *delouse*.
	3. Reduce; degrade: *declass*.
deca-, deka-	Ten: *decade*.
deci-	One tenth: *deciliter*.
demi-	Half; partly: *demigod*.
dendro-	Tree; treelike: *dendrochronology*.
denti-	Tooth; dental: *dentifrice*.
dextro-	On or to the right: *dextrorotatory*.
di-	Two; twice: *diacid*.
dia-, di-	Through; across: *diagonal*.
dis-	1. Not: *dissimilar*.
	2. Undo: *disarrange*.
	3. Used as an intensive: *disannul*.
dys-	Bad; impaired; abnormal: *dysfunction*.

146

ecto-	Outer; external: *ectoparasite*.
electro-	Electric: *electromagnet*.
en-[1], em-	1. To put or go into or on: *entrain*.
	2. To cause to be: *endear*.
	3. Thoroughly: *entangle*.
en-[2], em-	In; into; within: *enzootic*.
endo-	Inside; within: *endogenous*.
entero-	Intestine: *enteropathy*.
epi-	On: *epidermis*.
equi-	Equal; equally: *equidistant*.
ethno-	Race; people: *ethnology*.
eu-	Good: *eugenics*.
ex-, e-	Out of; away from: *exceed*.
extra-, extro-	Outside; beyond: *extraordinary*.
ferro-	Iron: *ferromagnetic*.
fibro-	Fiber; fibrous tissue: *fibroid*.
fore-	1. Before; earlier: *foredoom*.
	2. Front; in front of: *foredeck*.
geo-	Earth; geography: *geochronology*.
gyro-	Spinning; circle: *gyroscope*.
hecto-	One hundred: *hectogram*.
helio-	Sun: *heliograph*.
hemo-, hema-, hem-	Blood: *hemocyte*.
hepta-	Seven: *heptagon*.
hetero-	Other; different: *heterogynous*.
hexa-	Six: *hexagon*.
holo-	Whole; entire: *holography*.
homo-	Same; like: *homophone*.
hydro-	1. Water; liquid: *hydrodynamics*.
	2. Hydrogen: *hydrocarbon*.
hyper-	Over; beyond; excessive: *hypercritical*.
hypno-	1. Sleep: *hypnophobia*.
	2. Hypnosis: *hypnoanalysis*.
hypo-	Below; under: *hypodermic*.

147

ideo-	Idea: *ideomotor*.
in-[1], il-, im-, ir-	Not: *inarticulate*.
in-[2], il-, im-, ir-	In; into; within: *inbreed*.
inter-	Between; among: *international*.
intra-	Within: *intracellular*.
intro-	In; inward: *introjection*.
iso-	Equal; uniform: *isobar*.
kilo-	One thousand: *kilowatt*.
lacto-	Milk: *lactoprotein*.
leuko-, leuco-	White; colorless: *leukocyte*.
levo-	On or to the left: *levorotatory*.
litho-	Stone: *lithosphere*.
macro-	Large; long; inclusive: *macronucleus*.
magneto-	Magnetism; magnetic: *magnetoelectric*
mal-	Bad; abnormal: *maladminister*.
mega-	1. Large: *megaphone*.
	2. One million: *megahertz*.
meta-	1. Change: *metachromatism*.
	2. Beyond: *metalinguistics*.
micro-	1. Small: *microbiology*.
	2. One-millionth: *microcalorie*.
mid-	Middle: *midsummer*.
milli-	1. One-thousandth: *millisecond*.
	2. One thousand: *millipede*.
mis-	1. Bad; wrong; failure: *misconduct*.
	2. Used as an intensive: *misdoubt*.
mono-	One; single; alone: *monocline*.
multi-	Many; much; multiple: *multicolored*.
nano-	1. One-billionth: *nanosecond*.
	2. Extremely small: *nanoplankton*.
neo-	New; recent: *Neolithic*.
neuro-	Nerve; neural: *neurocyte*.
nitro-	Nitrogen: *nitrobacterium*.
non-	Not: *noncombatant*.

ob-	Inverse; inversely: *obcordate*.
octo-, octa-, oct-	Eight: *octane*.
oligo-	Few: *oligopoly*.
omni-	All: *omnidirectional*.
oo-	Egg; ovum: *oology*.
ortho-	Straight; correct: *orthodontia*.
paleo-	Ancient; early: *paleobotany*.
pan-	All; whole: *panorama*.
para-, par-	1. Beside; near: *parathyroid*.
	2. Beyond: *paranormal*.
	3. Resembling: *paratyphoid*.
	4. Subsidiary; assistant: *paraprofessional*.
pedo-	Child: *pedodontia*.
penta-	Five: *pentagon*.
per-	Thoroughly; completely; intensely: *perfervid*.
peri-	Around: *periscope*.
philo-	Loving: *philosophy*.
phono-	Sound; speech: *phonology*.
photo-	Light; radiant energy: *photosynthesis*.
physio-	Natural; physical: *physiography*.
phyto-	Plant: *phytogenesis*.
pico-	1. One-trillionth: *picosecond*.
	2. Very small: *picornavirus*.
poly-	Many; more than usual: *polychromatic*.
post-	After; behind: *postdoctoral*.
pre-	Earlier; before; in front of: *prehistoric*.
pro-[1]	Forward: *proceed*.
pro-[2]	Supporting: *prorevolutionary*.
pseudo-	False; deceptive: *pseudoscience*.
psycho-	Mind; mental; psychology: *psychogenic*.
pyro-	Fire; heat: *pyrotechnics*.
quadri, quadr-	Four: *quadrilateral*.
quasi-	In some manner: *quasi-scientific*.

re-	1. Again: *rebuild*.
	2. Back: *react*.
	3. Used as an intensive: *refine*.
retro-	Back: *retrograde*.
schizo-	Split: *schizophrenic*.
semi-	1. Half: *semicircle*.
	2. Partially: *semiconscious*.
	3. Resembling: *semiofficial*.
somn-	Sleep: *somnolence*.
spectro-	Spectrum: *spectrogram*.
spermato-	Sperm: *spermatocyte*.
spor-	Spore: *sporocyte*.
steno-	Narrow; small: *stenographer*.
stereo-	1. Solid: *stereotropism*.
	2. Three-dimensional: *stereoscopic*.
sub-	1. Below: *subsoil*.
	2. Secondary: *subplot*.
	3. Not completely: *subhuman*.
super-	1. Over: *superimpose*.
	2. Exceedingly: *superfine*.
sur-	1. Above: *surpass*.
	2. In addition: *surtax*.
syn-, sym-, syl-	Together: *synchronize*.
tele-	Distance: *television*.
tetra-	Four: *tetrahedron*.
theo-	God: *theology*.
thermo-	Heat: *thermodynamics*.
topo-	Place: *topography*.
tox-	Poison: *toxemia*.
trans-	1. Across; beyond: *transatlantic*.
	2. Change: *translate*.
tri-	Three: *triad*.
tricho-	Hair: *trichosis*.
ultra-	1. Beyond: *ultraviolet*.

	2. Excessively: *ultraconservative*.
un-[1]	1. Not: *unhappy*.
	2. The opposite of: *unrest*.
un-[2]	1. To reverse: *unbind*.
	2. Used as an intensive: *unloose*.
uni-	Single; one: *unicycle*.
up-	1. Up: *upheaval*.
	2. Upper: *upland*.
vaso-	Blood vessel: *vasodilator*.
veno-	Vein: *venous*.
xeno-	Stranger; foreigner: *xenophobic*.
xero-	Dry: *xeroderma*.
xylo-	Wood: *xylophone*.
zoo-	Animal: *zoology*.
zygo-	Paired: *zygomorphic*.

Suffixes

-able, -ible	Capable of: *debatable*.
-al	Of or relating to: *parental*.
-algia	Pain: *neuralgia*.
-an	Of or relating to: *librarian*.
-ance	State or action: *continuance*.
-ant	Causing or being: *deodorant*.
-ar	Of or relating to: *polar*.
-ate	Of or relating to: *collegiate*.
-chrome	Color: *monochrome*.
-cide	1. Killer: *insecticide*.
	2. Act of killing: *matricide*.
-cracy	Government: *democracy*.
-cy	1. State of being: *bankruptcy*.
	2. Rank: *baronetcy*.
-dom	1. Condition: *stardom*.
	2. Domain; rank: *dukedom*.
-ectomy	Surgical removal: *appendectomy*.

-ed	Having: *blackhearted*.
-eer	One concerned with: *profiteer*.
-en[1]	1. To cause to be: *cheapen*.
	2. To cause to have: *lengthen*.
-en[2]	Made of: *earthen*.
-ence	State or condition: *dependence*.
-ent	Causing or being: *absorbent*.
-er,-or	1. One that performs an action: *swimmer*.
	Native or resident of: *New Yorker*.
-ese	From or relating to: *Vietnamese*.
-ess	Female: *lioness*.
-est	Most: *nearest*.
-ferous	Being: *carboniferous*.
-ful	Full of: *playful*.
-fy	To cause to be: *electrify*.
-gamous	Marrying: *monogamous*.
-gamy	Marriage: *bigamy*.
-gram	Something written: *telegram*.
-graph	1. An instrument that writes: *seismograph*.
	2. Something written: *monograph*.
-hood	Condition or state: *manhood*.
-ia	Disease: *anorexia*.
-ian	Of or resembling: *Bostonian*.
-iatric	Relating to medical treatment: *geriatric*.
-iatry	Medical treatment: *psychiatry*.
-ic	Of or relating to: *Icelandic*.
-ine	Of or resembling: *canine*.
-ing	Used to form the present participle: *singing*.
-ion	Act or process: *admission*.
-ish	1. Of or like: *childish*.
	2. Tending toward: *greenish*.
-ism	1. Action or process: *terrorism*.
	2. Characteristic behavior: *heroism*.
	3. Doctrine; theory: *pacifism*.

-ist	1. One that produces: *novelist*.
	2. A specialist: *biologist*.
	3. An adherent of a doctrine: *anarchist*.
-ite	1. A native of: *New Jerseyite*.
	2. One associated with: *socialite*.
-itis	Inflammation or disease: *laryngitis*.
-ive	Of or tending toward: *demonstrative*.
-ize, -ise	1. To cause to be: *dramatize*.
	2. To become: *materialize*.
	3. To treat with: *anesthetize*.
-lepsy	Seizure: *epilepsy*.
-less	Without: *blameless*.
-let	Small: *booklet*.
-lith	Stone: *monolith*.
-logy	1. Science: *biology*.
	2. Discourse: *phraseology*.
-ly	Like: *friendly*.
-mania	Exaggerated enthusiasm: *pyromania*.
-ment	1. Action or process: *appeasement*.
	2. Result of an action or process: *advance-ment*.
-meter	A measuring device: *pedometer*.
-metry	Science of measuring: *geometry*.
-most	Most: *innermost*.
-ness	State; quality: *brightness*.
-nomy	A body of knowledge: *astronomy*.
-oid	Resembling: *spheroid*.
-opsy	Examination: *biopsy*.
-osis	Abnormal condition: *neurosis*.
-ous	Characterized by: *joyous*.
-sect	To cut: *bisect*.
-ship	1. State or condition: *scholarship*.
	2. Rank or office: *professorship*.
-some	Characterized by: *bothersome*.

-stat	A stabilizing instrument: *thermostat*.
-tion	Act or process: *absorption*.
-tomy	Act of cutting: *lobotomy*.
-tude	Condition or state: *exactitude*.
-ule	Small: *globule*.
-ure	Act or process: *failure*.
-ward	In a direction: *downward*.
-wise	1. In a manner or direction: *clockwise*.
	2. In regard to: *dollarwise*.

FOREIGN WORDS AND PHRASES

The English language has grown by incorporating words from many of the world's different languages. There remain, however, many words and phrases used in English that retain a distinctly foreign flavor. The following list contains the most common words and phrases that you are likely to encounter. Latin terms are marked (L) and French terms (F).

à bon marché (F)	At a bargain price
annus mirabilis (L)	A year of wonders or disasters
à propos de rien (F)	Apropos of nothing
au contraire (F)	On the contrary
au fait (F)	Skilled or knowledgeable
aurea mediocritas (L)	The golden mean
au revoir (F)	Good-by
aussitôt dit, aussitôt fait (F)	No sooner said than done
autre temps, autres moeurs (F)	Other times, other customs

ave atque vale (L)	Hail and farewell
avec plaisir (F)	With pleasure
bête noire (F)	Something or someone that one particularly dislikes
bona fide (L)	In good faith; genuine
bon jour (F)	Good day; hello
bon soir (F)	Good evening; good night
carpe diem (L)	Enjoy the present
casus belli (L)	An event justifying a declaration of war
causa sine qua non (L)	An indispensable condition
caveat emptor (L)	Let the buyer beware
cave canem (L)	Beware of the dog
c'est-à-dire (F)	That is to say
c'est la vie (F)	Such is life
chacun à son goût (F)	Everyone to his own taste
chef de cuisine (F)	Head cook
cherchez la femme (F)	Look for the woman
cogito ergo sum (L)	I think, therefore I am
compte rendu (F)	Report; account
coûte que coûte (F)	Cost what it may
degustibus non est disputandum (L)	There is no arguing about tastes
Dei gratia (L)	By the grace of God
Deo gratias (L)	Thanks be to God
Deo volente (L)	God willing
de trop (F)	Too much or too many; superfluous
Deus vobiscum (L)	God be with you
Dieu avec nous (F)	God with us
Dieu defend le droit (F)	God defends the right
Dieu et mon droit (F)	God and my right
Dominus vobiscum (L)	The Lord be with you
dulce et decorum est pro patria mori (L)	It is sweet and fitting to die for one's country
ecce homo (L)	Behold the man

en famille (F)	In one's family; informally
en plein jour (F)	In full daylight; openly
en rapport (F)	In sympathy or accord
e pluribus unum (L)	One out of many
ex cathedra (L)	With the authority derived from one's office
ex more (L)	According to custom
fait accompli (F)	An accomplished fact or deed
femme de chambre (F)	A chambermaid
festina lente (L)	Make haste slowly
gaudeamus igitur (L)	Let us then be joyful
genius loci (L)	Guardian deity; the distinctive character of a place
hic sepultus (L)	Here lies buried
hinc illae lacrimae (L)	Hence those tears
hoc anno (L)	In this year
honi soit qui mal y pense (F)	Shame to him who thinks evil of it
humanum est errare (L)	To err is human
in extremis (L)	At the point of death
in loco parentis (L)	In the place of a parent
in medias res (L)	In or into the middle of a sequence of events
in omnia paratus (L)	Prepared for all things
in perpetuum (L)	Forever
in propria persona (L)	In one's own person
in rerum natura (L)	In the nature of things
in situ (L)	In its place
in statu quo ante (L)	In the state in which it was before
integer vitae scelerisque purus (L)	Upright in life and free from wickedness
in toto (L)	Altogether; entirely
in vino veritas (L)	There is truth in wine
ipso jure (L)	By the law itself
jure divino (L)	By divine law
jus canonicum (L)	Canon law

justitia omnibus (L)	Justice for all
j'y suis, j'y reste (F)	Here I am, here I stay
labor omnia vincit (L)	Work conquers all things
laus Deo (L)	Praise be to God
le roi est mort, vive le roi (F)	The king is dead! Long live the king!
le style, c'est l'homme (F)	The style is the man
le tout ensemble (F)	The whole (taken) together
locus in quo (L)	The place in which
loquitur (L)	He or she speaks
ma foi (F)	Really!
mal de mer (F)	Seasickness
mal du pays (F)	Homesickness
mens sana in corpore sano (L)	A sound mind in a healthy body
miles gloriosus (L)	A bragging soldier
mirable dictu (L)	Wonderful to say
mirabilia (L)	Miracles
mise en scène (F)	A stage setting; environment
modus operandi (L)	Method of operating
mon ami (F)	My friend
morituri te salutamus (L)	We who are about to die salute you
mutatis mutandis (L)	The necessary changes having been made
nemine contradicente (L)	No one contradicting
nemine dissentiente (L)	No one dissenting
n'est-ce pas? (F)	Isn't that so?
nolens volens (L)	Whether willing or not
nom de guerre (F)	A pseudonym
non possumus (L)	We are not able
obiit (L)	He or she died
objet d'art (F)	A work of art
omnia vincit amor (L)	Love conquers all
opere citato (L)	In the work cited
O tempora! O mores! (L)	O times! O customs!

pari passu (L)	With equal pace
pax vobiscum (L)	Peace be with you
persona grata (L)	Fully acceptable
pièce de résistance (F)	An outstanding accomplishment
pied-à-terre (F)	A secondary or temporary lodging
pis aller (F)	The last resort
pleno jure (L)	With full authority
plus ça change, plus c'est la même chose (F)	The more it changes, the more it's the same thing
primus inter pares (L)	First among equals
pro bono publico (L)	For the public good
pro forma (L)	Done in a perfunctory way
pro rege, lege, et grege (L)	For the king, the law, and the people
pro tempore (L)	For the time being; temporarily
qui s'excuse, s'accuse (F)	He who excuses himself accuses himself
quod vide (L)	Which see
quo jure? (L)	By what right?
quot homines, quot sententiae (L)	There are as many opinions as there are men
raison d'état (F)	For the good of the country
raison d'être (F)	Reason for existing
requiescat in pace (L)	May he or she rest in peace
sans doute (F)	Without doubt
sans gene (F)	Without embarrassment
sans pareil (F)	Without equal
sans peine (F)	Without difficulty
sans peur et sans reproche (F)	Without fear and without reproach
sans souci (F)	Carefree
scripsit (L)	He or she wrote (it)
sculpsit (L)	He or she sculptured (it)
secundum (L)	According to
semper idem (L)	Always the same

semper paratus (L)	Always ready
sic itur ad astra (L)	Thus one goes to the stars
sic passim (L)	Thus throughout
sic semper tyrannis (L)	Thus always to tyrants
sic transit gloria mundi (L)	Thus passes away the glory of the world
sine die (L)	Without a day specified for a future meeting
sine qua non (L)	Something essential
splendide mendax (L)	Nobly untruthful
sub verbo (L)	Under the word
summum bonum (L)	The greatest good
suo jure (L)	In one's own right
suo loco (L)	In one's rightful place
suum cuique (L)	To each his own
tant mieux (F)	So much the better
tant pis (F)	So much the worse
tempora mutantur, nos et mutamur in illis (L)	Times change, and we change with them
tempus fugit (L)	Time flies
timeo Danaos et dona ferentes (L)	I fear the Greeks even when they bear gifts
ut infra (L)	As below
up supra (L)	As above
vade mecum (L)	Go with me; guidebook
vae victis (L)	Woe to the conquered
vale (L)	Farewell
verbatim et literatim (L)	Word for word and letter for letter
voilà (F)	Look! See!

159

How it is
Written

FORMS OF ADDRESS

Forms of address do not always follow set guidelines; the type of salutation is often determined by the relationship between correspondents or by the purpose and content of the letter. However, a general style applies to most occasions. In formal salutations, when the addressee is a woman, "Madam," should be substituted for "Sir." When the salutation is informal, "Mrs.," or "Miss" or "Ms." should be substituted for "Mr." If a woman addressee has previously stated a preference for a particular form of address this form should be used.

	Form of Address	Salutation
Academics		
assistant professor, college or university	Dr. (or Mr.) Joseph Stone Assistant Professor Department of _____	Dear Professor Stone:
associate professor, college or university	Dr. (or Mr.) Joseph Stone Associate Professor Department of _____	Dear Professor Stone:
chancellor, university	Chancellor Joseph Stone	Dear Chancellor Stone:

dean college or university	Dean Joseph Stone *or* Dr. (*or* Mr.) Joseph Stone Dean, School of ———	Dear Dean Stone: Dear Dr. (*or* Mr.) Stone:
president, college or university	President Joseph Stone *or* Dr. (*or* Mr.) Joseph Stone President, ———	Dear President Stone: Dear Dr. (*or* Mr.) Stone:
professor, college or university	Professor Joseph Stone *or* Dr. (*or* Mr.) Joseph Stone Department of ———	Dear Professor Stone: Dear Dr. (*or* Mr.) Stone:

Clerical and Religious Orders

abbot, Roman Catholic	The Right Reverend Joseph Stone, O.S.B. Abbot of ———	Right Reverend Abbot:
archbishop, Armenian Church	His Eminence the Archbishop of ———	Your Eminence: *or* Your Excellency:
archbishop, Greek Orthodox	His Eminence Archbishop Joseph Stone	Your Eminence:
archbishop, Roman Catholic	The Most Reverend Joseph Stone Archbishop of ———	Your Excellency:

163

archbishop, Russian Orthodox	His Eminence the Archbishop of ⎯⎯⎯⎯ *or* The Most Reverend Archbishop of ⎯⎯⎯⎯	Your Grace: Right Reverend Joseph:
archdeacon, Episcopal	The Venerable Joseph Stone, Archdeacon of ⎯⎯⎯⎯	Venerable Sir: Dear Archdeacon Stone: Dear Father Stone:
archimandrite, Russian Orthodox	Very Reverend Father Joseph Stone	Very Reverend Father: Very Reverend Father Stone:
archpriest, Russian Orthodox	Very Reverend Father Joseph Stone	Very Reverend Father: Very Reverend Father Stone:
bishop, Episcopal	The Right Reverend Joseph Stone Bishop of ⎯⎯⎯⎯	Right Reverend Sir: Dear Bishop Stone:
bishop, Greek Orthodox	The Right Reverend Joseph Stone	Your Grace:
bishop, Methodist	Bishop Joseph Stone	Dear Bishop Stone:
bishop, Roman Catholic	The Most Reverend Joseph Stone Bishop of ⎯⎯⎯⎯	Your Excellency:
brotherhood, Roman Catholic, member of	Brother Joseph Stone, C.F.C.	Dear Brother: Dear Brother Joseph:
canon, Episcopal	The Reverend Canon Joseph Stone	Dear Canon Stone:

cantor	Cantor Joseph Stone	Dear Cantor Stone:
cardinal	His Eminence Joseph Cardinal Stone	Your Eminence:
clergyman, Protestant	The Reverend Joseph Stone *or* The Reverend Joseph Stone, D.D.	Dear Mr. (or Dr.) Stone:
elder, Presbyterian	Elder Joseph Stone	Dear Elder Stone:
dean of a cathedral, Episcopal	The Very Reverend Joseph Stone Dean of ____	Very Reverend Sir: Dear Dean Stone:
metropolitan, Russian Orthodox	His Eminence the Metropolitan of ____ *or* The Most Reverend Metropolitan of ____	Your Grace: Right Reverend Joseph:
monsignor, Roman Catholic	Reverend Monsignor Joseph Stone	Reverend Monsignor: Dear Monsignor: Dear Monsignor Stone:
patriarch, Armenian Church	His Beatitude the Patriarch of ____	Your Beatitude:
patriarch, Greek Orthodox	His All Holiness Patriarch Demetrios	Your All Holiness:
patriarch, Russian Orthodox	His Beatitude the Patriarch of ____	Your Beatitude:

pope	His Holiness Pope John XXIII *or* His Holiness the Pope	Your Holiness:
president, Mormon Church	President Joseph Stone Church of Jesus Christ of Latter-day Saints	Dear President Stone:
priest, Greek Orthodox	Reverend Father Joseph Stone	Dear Reverend Stone: Dear Reverend Father:
priest, Roman Catholic	The Reverend Joseph Stone, S.J.	Dear Reverend Father: Dear Father: Dear Father Stone:
priest, Russian Orthodox	The Reverend Joseph Stone	Reverend Father: Reverend Father Stone:
protopresbyter, Russian Orthodox	Very Reverend Father Joseph Stone	Very Reverend Father: Very Reverend Father Stone:
rabbi	Rabbi Joseph Stone *or* Joseph Stone, D.D.	Dear Rabbi (*or* Dr.) Stone:
sisterhood, Roman Catholic, member of	Sister Mary Stone, C.S.J.	Dear Sister: Dear Sister Mary:
supreme patriarch, Armenian Church	His Holiness the Supreme Patriarch and Catholicos of all Armenians	Your Holiness:

Diplomats

ambassador, U.S.	The Honorable Joseph Stone The Ambassador of the United States	Sir: Dear Mr. Ambassador:
ambassador to the U.S.	His Excellency Joseph Stone The Ambassador of ____	Excellency: Dear Mr. Ambassador:
chargé d'affaires, U.S.	Joseph Stone, Esq. American Chargé d'Affaires	Dear Sir:
chargé d'affaires, to the U.S.	Joseph Stone, Esq. Chargé d'Affaires of ____	Dear Sir:
consul, U.S.	Mr. Joseph Stone American Consul	Sir: Dear Mr. Consul:
minister, U.S.	The Honorable Joseph Stone The Minister of the United States	Sir: Dear Mr. Minister:
minister to the U.S.	The Honorable Joseph Stone The Minister of ____	Sir: Dear Mr. Minister:
secretary general, United Nations	His Excellency Joseph Stone Secretary General of the United Nations	Excellency: Dear Mr. Secretary General:
U.S. representative to the United Nations	The Honorable Joseph Stone United States Representative to the United Nations	Sir: Dear Mr. Stone:

167

Federal, state, and local officials (government)

alderman	The Honorable Joseph Stone	Dear Mr. Stone:
assistant to the President	The Honorable Joseph Stone Assistant to the President The White House	Dear Mr. Stone:
Attorney General, U.S.	The Honorable Joseph Stone Attorney General of the United States	Dear Mr. Attorney General:
attorney general, state	The Honorable Joseph Stone Attorney General State of _____	Dear Mr. Attorney General:
assemblyman, state	The Honorable Joseph Stone Assembly State Capitol	Dear Mr. Stone:
cabinet member	The Honorable Joseph Stone Secretary of _____	Dear Mr. Secretary:
assistant secretary of a department	The Honorable Joseph Stone Assistant Secretary of _____	Dear Mr. Stone:
undersecretary of a department	The Honorable Joseph Stone Undersecretary of _____	Dear Mr. Stone:
deputy secretary of a department	The Honorable Joseph Stone Deputy Secretary of _____	Dear Mr. Stone:

168

chairman, House Committee	The Honorable Joseph Stone Chairman, Committee on ——— United States House of Representatives	Dear Mr. Chairman:
chairman, joint committee of Congress	The Honorable Joseph Stone Chairman, Joint Committee on ——— Congress of the United States	Dear Mr. Chairman:
chairman, Senate Committee	The Honorable Joseph Stone Chairman, Committee on ——— United States Senate	Dear Mr. Chairman:
chief justice, U.S. Supreme Court	The Chief Justice of the United States The Supreme Court of the United States	Dear Mr. Chief Justice:
associate justice, U.S. Supreme Court	Mr. Justice Stone The Supreme Court of the United States	Dear Mr. Justice:
commissioner (federal, state, or local)	The Honorable Joseph Stone	Dear Mr. Stone:
delegate, state	The Honorable Joseph Stone ——— House of Delegates State Capitol	Dear Mr. Stone:
governor	The Honorable Joseph Stone Governor of ———	Dear Governor Stone:
judge, federal	The Honorable Joseph Stone Judge of the United States Tax Court	Dear Judge Stone:

169

judge, state or local	The Honorable Joseph Stone Judge of the Superior Court of _____	Dear Judge Stone:
lieutenant governor	The Honorable Joseph Stone Lieutenant Governor of _____	Dear Mr. Stone:
mayor	The Honorable Joseph Stone Mayor of _____	Dear Mayor Stone:
Postmaster General	The Honorable Joseph Stone Postmaster General of the United States	Dear Mr. Postmaster General:
President, U.S.	The President The White House	Dear Mr. President:
former President, U.S.	The Honorable Joseph Stone	Dear Mr. Stone:
representative, state	The Honorable Joseph Stone House of Representatives State Capitol	Dear Mr. Stone:
representative, U.S.	The Honorable Joseph Stone United States House of Representatives	Dear Mr. Stone:
secretary of state, state	The Honorable Joseph Stone Secretary of State State Capitol	Dear Mr. Secretary:
senator, state	The Honorable Joseph Stone The State Senate State Capitol	Dear Senator Stone:

senator, U.S.	The Honorable Joseph Stone United States Senate	Dear Senator Stone:
Speaker, U.S. House of Representatives	The Honorable Joseph Stone Speaker of the House of Representatives	Dear Mr. Speaker:
Vice President, U.S.	The Vice President United States Senate	Dear Mr. Vice President:

Professions

attorney	Mr. Joseph Stone Attorney at Law *or* Joseph Stone, Esq.	Dear Mr. Stone:
chiropractor	Joseph Stone, D.C. (office) *or* Dr. Joseph Stone (residence)	Dear Dr. Stone:
dentist	Joseph Stone, D.D.S. (office) *or* Dr. Joseph Stone (residence)	Dear Dr. Stone:
physician	Joseph Stone, M.D. (office) *or* Dr. Joseph Stone (residence)	Dear Dr. Stone:
veterinarian	Joseph Stone, D.V.M. (office) *or* Dr. Joseph Stone (residence)	Dear Dr. Stone:

Military

admiral vice admiral rear admiral	Full rank, full name, abbreviation of service branch	Dear Admiral Stone:
airman first class airman airman basic	Full rank, full name, abbreviation of service branch	Dear Airman Stone:
cadet (air force, army)	Cadet Joseph Stone United States Air Force Academy United States Military Academy	Dear Cadet Stone: *or* Dear Mr. Stone:
captain, (air force, army, coast guard, marine corps, navy)	Full rank, full name, abbreviation of service branch	Dear Captain Stone:
chief petty officer (coast guard, navy)	Full rank, full name, abbreviation of service branch	Dear Mr. Stone: *or* Dear Chief Stone:
chief warrant officer, warrant officer (air force, army, marine corps, navy)	Full rank, full name, abbreviation of service branch	Dear Mr. Stone:
colonel, lieutenant	Full rank, full name.	Dear Colonel Stone:

	abbreviation of service branch	
colonel (air force, army, marine corps)	abbreviation of service branch	Dear Commander Stone:
commander (coast guard, navy)	Full rank, full name, abbreviation of service branch	Dear Commodore Stone:
commodore (navy)	Full rank, full name, abbreviation of service branch	Dear Corporal Stone:
corporal (army), lance corporal (marine corps)	Full rank, full name, abbreviation of service branch	Dear Mr. Stone: *or* Dear Ensign Stone:
ensign (coast guard, navy)	Full rank, full name, abbreviation of service branch	Dear Lieutenant Stone:
first lieutenant, second lieutenant (air force, army, marine corps)	Full rank, full name, abbreviation of service branch	Dear General Stone:
general, lieutenant general, major general, brigadier general (air force, army, marine corps)	Full rank, full name, abbreviation of service branch	Dear Mr. Stone:
lieutenant commander,	Full rank, full name,	

Rank	Address form	Salutation
lieutenant, lieutenant (jg) (coast guard, navy)	abbreviation of service branch	*or* Dear Lieutenant Stone:
major (air force, army, marine corps)	Full rank, full name, abbreviation of service branch	Dear Major Stone:
midshipman	Midshipman Joseph Stone United States Coast Guard Academy United States Naval Academy	Dear Midshipman Stone:
petty officer (coast guard, navy)	Full rank, full name, abbreviation of service branch	Dear Mr. Stone:
private first class, private (air force, army, marine corps)	Full rank, full name, abbreviation of service branch	Dear Private Stone:
seaman, seaman apprentice, seaman recruit (coast guard, navy)	Full rank, full name, abbreviation of service branch	Dear Seaman Stone:
master sergeant (air force, army, marine corps)	Full rank, full name, abbreviation of service branch	Dear Sergeant Stone:

Note: Other compound titles in enlisted ranks are not shown here. They all follow forms indicated for this example

Rank	Address form	Salutation
specialist (army)	Full rank, full name, abbreviation of service branch	Dear Specialist Stone:

THE RÉSUMÉ

A résumé is a short description of your history in work and at school. Many white-collar jobs require a résumé from any prospective employee. At times, your résumé will be mailed to a prospective employer. What the résumé reveals about you may determine whether or not you are actually interviewed for a job.

The résumé should be neatly typed. If you are not a good typist, there are services that will retype the material you have written. Spelling and grammar should be correct. It is advisable to have someone else read over what you have written before you send it out. Once you are satisfied that what you have written is in good order, you will want to have copies made. Copies should be made on good quality paper. There are many small shops that reproduce résumés by photo offset or xerography. It is not in your best interest to send out copies of your résumé on the gray or pink slippery paper available in many library duplicating machines.

Format

Résumés have a fairly standard format. At the very top, give your name, address, and telephone number. Many people include their age and marital status, although it is not necessary to include them. You must judge whether your age and marital status will assist you in your job search or work against you.

The next item in the résumé is a brief paragraph that may be labeled "Objectives." In the paragraph, you indicate what job you are looking for and your major qualifications for such a job. Or you may simply use this paragraph to state your basic strengths and the nature of your past work.

Following this is the record of your work experience. This record is the main part of the résumé (except if you are looking for your first full-time job). Your work experience is listed with your most recent job first. The job before that is listed next, and so on with your first job listed last:

1977 to present
1973 to 1977
1970 to 1973

Usually, you give your title for each job and the name of the company (and division when relevant). Sometimes you may not want to reveal the name of your current employer in your résumé. Then you may write a descriptive phrase, such as "independent engineering consultant firm."

Résumés are generally kept to one page. If you have worked for a very long time at a variety of different jobs, it may be necessary to prepare a two-page résumé.

After the record of your work experience, list your schooling, any degrees, relevant noncredit courses, hobbies, honors, and affiliations that you consider worth including. For example, physical fitness is an asset: if you jog, swim, play tennis or golf, or engage in any other fitness activity, it may be worth noting. If you belong to professional societies, you should definitely list them. If you belong to social, civic, or volunteer organizations, list them only if you believe your membership in them is an asset. Do list any awards or honors you have received whether or not they are job-related. Such honors indicate that you are esteemed by others.

Looking for Your First Job

If you are looking for your first full-time job, you must review your work history somewhat differently. If you have held some sort of part-time or summer job or worked at volunteer jobs, these should be included. If you have participated in school extracurricular activities, these are worth mentioning. Your school record is also an indication of your ability and seriousness of purpose.

In seeking a first job, you must state your field of knowledge, that you are reliable, and that you can work well with others.

Whether you are looking for your first job or your fourth job, the time span from the end of schooling to the present should be accounted for on your résumé. You may be sure that a gap of a year or two will be noticed. If you have taken off a year and traveled around the world, say so. If you have attempted unsuccessfully to start your own business, say so. It is far better than allowing a prospective employer to wonder what you were doing with your time.

Below are two sample résumés. The first is for a person looking for a first job. The second résumé is for a person who has held several jobs. The résumé indicates that each job has involved more responsibility and skills than the previous job.

Leslie White
987 East Road
Elmwood, New Jersey 03103
987-6543

Objective

To find an entry-level job in sales with a large international company. Would like to utilize my knowledge of French.

Work experience

Summers 1978, 1977

Group leader in a European teen-travel summer trip. We traveled on bicycles and by boat. Many of the arrangements had been made in advance, but I often had to make substitute arrangements because of unforeseen events.

Summer 1976

Spent three months in France working as a volunteer on a farm. Did so to improve my spoken French.

Part-time employment 1977, 1978, 1979

Salesperson, college bookstore during school year.

School record

1979
B.A. magna cum laude with honors in French Literature and Language. Minor in History. Princeton University.

1975
Elmwood High School, class salutatorian. Honors in language and science.

Extracurricular activities

Member of soccer team in high school and college.
Contributor to school magazine in college.
President of French Club in high school.

Speak and write French fluently. Have working knowledge of Spanish.

Courtney Black
123 Lincoln Street
Deerfield, Illinois 60015
789-3456

Objectives

To find a job that would utilize a broad range of my managerial and business skills and offer the potential for advancement in a large company.

Record of work experience

1977 to present
Public Relations Director for a small manufacturing company

Am responsible for creating and maintaining a favorable public image by preparing and disseminating news releases, arranging press conferences, contests, conferences, and other activities that keep the company in the public eye. Supervise a staff of six and work with various other departments: art, advertising, production, etc. Maintain close working relations with various people in the media and local government.

1973 to 1977
Publicity Writer for the Widget Company

Wrote copy for publicity releases and other public-relations material. Know paper, printing, art styles. Many of my releases appeared in trade journals and local newspapers. Two-person office made for more responsibility than a publicity writer normally encounters.

1970 to 1973
Copy editor for Deerfield Gazette

Corrected copy and did proofreading for the local paper. Did some rewrite and occasional reporting.

Educational background

M.B.A. University of Illinois, 1976. Took night courses for master's degree.

B.A. University of Illinois, 1970. Major in Journalism. Received award for Most Promising Student.

Extracurricular: Worked on college newspaper; member of swim team.

Affiliations and hobbies

Member of Illinois Society of Publicity Writers

Vice President of Alumni Association, University of Illinois

Hobbies include swimming, tennis, and directing amateur theater productions.

The Cover Letter

A résumé that will be mailed to a prospective employer should be accompanied by a cover letter. The cover letter should be straightforward and brief; it should not be a repetition of all the information contained in the résumé. You should state the specific position you are interested in, briefly discuss your experience, and refer the reader to the enclosed résumé. At the end of the letter you may wish to indicate that you will telephone the prospective employer for an interview.

You will, of course, have to write a separate cover letter for each specific position you want to apply for. The cover letter, like the résumé, should be neatly typed and quality paper should be used. Remember that the cover letter serves as your introduction to a prospective employer and that first impressions are very important. Be sure that the spelling and grammar are correct and that you have spelled all names and addresses properly.

Dear Sirs:

I am applying for the position of assistant sales manager, advertised in Sunday's Boston Globe. I have held a number of selling jobs and am currently working in the sales department of a large manufacturing company.

The enclosed résumé will furnish additional information on my background. I will telephone you next week for an interview. Thank you for your consideration.

Sincerely,

Ellen Kovalcik

Ms. Ellen Kovalcik

BUSINESS LETTERS

The formats of the following four letters are typical of those used in business correspondence, although other variations certainly exist. For example, in the sample executive letter the date could have been centered on the page instead of aligned with the right-hand margin.

Most letters are single-spaced, with double spacing between paragraphs. In the full block and modified block formats the first line of each paragraph aligns with the left-hand margin. In the modified semiblock and executive formats the first line is indented five to ten spaces.

When stationery without a printed letterhead is used, the mailing address of the sender is typed in two lines, centered, at the top of the page:

9988 Beacon Street
New York, New York 12345

Full Block

1 15 Lines 2 4, 6, or 8 Lines 3 Double Spaces 4 4 Lines 5 Copy notation
6 Enclosure notation 7 Identifying Initials 8 Writer's Name and Title
9 Complimentary Close 10 Body of Letter 11 Salutation 12 Inside Address 13 Date

Houghton Mifflin Company

One Beacon Street. Boston. Massachusetts 02108
(617) 725-5000 Cable HOUGHTON

Trade & Reference Division

1

13   April 3, 19--

2

12   Ms. Jennifer Stone
     Vice President, Corporate Plans
     CBA Corporation
     43 Hunting Towers, Suite 100
     Jonesville, ST 98765

11   Dear Ms. Stone:

     This is the Block letter, all elements of which are aligned tight
     with the left margin. Spacing between letter parts is indicated
     by the key lines. Individual paragraphs in the message are
     single-spaced internally. Double-spacing separates each of the
10   paragraphs.

     If the letter exceeds one page, a continuation sheet may be used.
     The heading begins six lines from the top edge of the page. The
     heading includes the name of the addressee, the date, and the
     page number, blocked and aligned tight with the left margin as
     shown below:

     Ms. Stone
     Page 2
     April 3, 19--

     The message continues four lines below the heading. At least
     three message lines must be carried over to the continuation
     sheet: the complimentary close and the signature block should
     never stand alone there.

     The writer's corporate title is shown under the typewritten
     signature. Typist's initials, enclosure notations, and carbon
     copy recipients are typewritten tight with the left margin and
     are spaced as shown by the key lines.

9   Sincerely yours,

     John B. Brown   4

8   John B. Brown
     Director of Marketing

7   JBB: ahs
6   enclosures (2)

     cc: S.A. Langhorne

     5

Atlanta Dallas Geneva Illinois Lawrenceville New Jersey Palo Alto London

3

Modified Block

1 15 Lines **2** Date **3** 4, 6, or 8 Lines **4** Double Spaces **5** 4 Lines **6** Copy notation **7** Enclosure notation **8** Identifying Initials **9** Writer's Name and Title **10** Complimentary Close **11** Body of Letter **12** Subject Line **13** Salutation **14** Inside Address

Houghton Mifflin Company

One Beacon Street, Boston, Massachusetts 02108
(617) 725-5000   Cable HOUGHTON

Trade & Reference Division

2

April 3, 19--

1

3

Mr. Irwin A. Levine
Treasurer, CCC Corporation
14 123 Westwood Blvd.
Jonesville, ST 98765

13 Dear Mr. Levine:

12 Subject: Modified Block Letter

This is the Modified Block Letter. Its distinctive features are:
a date line, a complimentary close, and a signature block aligned
slightly to the right of center-page, as shown here, or aligned
tight with the right margin. A subject line, if included, is
centered on the page.

4

11 The inside address, salutation message, typist's initials,
enclosure notations, and list of carbon copy recipients are
aligned tight with the left margin. If the message exceeds one
page, a continuation sheet is used. The continuation sheet
heading is typed six lines from the top edge of the page. It may
be blocked and aligned tight with the left margin, as shown
within the Block Letter, or it may be spaced across the page on a
single line, as

Mr. Levine   -2-   April 3, 19--

At least three message lines must be carried over to the
continuation sheet; the complimentary close and the signature
block must never stand alone there.

Spacing between all elements of the Modified Block Letter is
indicated by the key lines.

10 Very truly yours,

Nora A. Martin

5

Nora A. Martin
9 Comptroller

8 NAM: ahs
7 encs: 5

CC: L.A. Long
     J.A. Matthews
6 → M.M. Smith
     T.C. Vickers

Atlanta Dallas Geneva Illinois Lawrenceville New Jersey Palo Alto London

Modified Semiblock

1 15 Lines **2** Date **3** 4, 6, or 8 Lines **4** Double Spaces **5** 4 Lines **6** Identifying Initials **7** Writer's Name and Title **8** Complimentary Close **9** Body of Letter **10** Salutation **11** Subject Line **12** Attention Line **13** Inside Address

Houghton Mifflin Company

One Beacon Street, Boston, Massachusetts 02108
(617) 725-5000   Cable HOUGHTON

Trade & Reference Division

2

1

April 3, 19—

3

13 3L Typesetters, Inc.
123 Industrial Park Road
Jonesville, ST 98765

12 Attention: John Hodges

   11 Subject: Modified Semiblock Letter

10 Gentlemen:

   This is an example of the Modified Semiblock Letter. Its date line,
complimentary close, and signature block may be typed slightly to the right
of center-page or they may be positioned tight with the right margin, as
shown here. The inside address, salutation, and typist's initials are
placed flush with the left margin. An attention line, if used, is placed
flush left. A subject line, if used, is centered on the page.

   9   Individual paragraphs of the Modified Semiblock Letter may be indented
by five or ten character spaces. Carried over lines are aligned tight with
the left margin. Double spacing separates the single-spaced paragraphs.

   If the letter exceeds one page, a continuation sheet is used. At
least three message lines should be carried over to the continuation sheet;   **4**
at no time should the complimentary close and the signature block stand
alone there.

   Continuation sheet headings in this letter style are typewritten
across the top of the page, six lines from the edge, as shown in the
Modified Block facsimile. The message continues four lines below the
heading.

   If a postscript is added to the letter, it too is indented by five to
ten character spaces so as to align with the message paragraphs.

                              8 Sincerely,

                                 Lee Matthews

                              7 Lee Matthews   **5**
                                 Editor

LM: ahs

   6 It is not necessary to introduce a postscript with the abbreviation
P.S., but the writer should initial the postscript, as shown here.
                                 L.M.

Atlanta Dallas Geneva Illinois Lawrenceville New Jersey Palo Alto London

187

Executive

1 15 Lines 2 Date 3 4 to 10 Lines 4 Double Spaces 5 4 Lines 6 4 Lines
7 Enclosure Notation 8 Identifying initials 9 Inside Address 10 Title of
Writer 11 Complimentary Close 12 Body of Letter 13 Salutation

Houghton Mifflin Company

One Beacon Street, Boston, Massachusetts 02108
(617) 725-5000   Cable HOUGHTON

Trade & Reference Division

2

1

April 3, 19--

3

13 Dear Mr. Fitzpatrick:

    This is the Executive Letter. In this styling, the inside
address appears from two to five lines below the last line of the
signature block, depending on the length of the message. It is
aligned tight with the left margin.

    The date line appears flush with the right margin. The
paragraphs are indented from five to ten character spaces, and
12 lines that are carried over are aligned flush left. Paragraphs
are single-spaced internally. Double spacing separates one
paragraph from another.

    The complimentary close is aligned under the date, tight
with the right margin. A typewritten signature block is
unnecessary if the writer's name and title are already included
in the printed corporate letterhead.

4

    If the typist's initials and other notations are included,
they appear two lines beneath the last line of the inside
address.

11 Sincerely,

10 Michael A. Robb
       Director

5

6

John X. Fitzpatrick, Esq.
9 Fitzpatrick, Swanson, and Norton
Two Court Street
Jonesville, ST 98765

8 MAR: ahs

Enclosure

7

Atlanta Dallas Geneva Illinois Lawrenceville New Jersey Palo Alto London

MINUTES OF MEETINGS

Format

Minutes are a brief and official record of the meeting of a group. They are prepared either by a recording secretary or by a specially designated member of the group.

Depending upon the group or the nature of the meeting, minutes may be formal or informal. Many organizations have preferred formats for minutes, and certain kinds of meetings, such as directors' or stockholders' meetings, have specific required formats. Regardless of the format, the following information is always included.

1. Name of the group.
2. Type of meeting: regular, special, etc.
3. Date, time, and place.
4. Names of those present and absent.
5. Name of presiding officer and recording secretary.
6. Proceedings:
   a. Presentation, amendments (if necessary), and approval of previous minutes.
   b. Unfinished business.
   c. New business.
7. Date of next meeting.
8. Hour of adjournment.
9. Signature of secretary.

Style

In preparing minutes you should keep the exact wording of resolutions and motions passed and the names of the proposers. Reports that are appended to the minutes or kept separate may be summarized. Frequently you will find it helpful to summarize the discussion.

It is important to remember that in addition to informing absent members of what took place at a meeting, minutes are an official record that may subsequently be referred to for a variety of purposes. Therefore they must be written cogently and accurately. Even though minutes present only the crucial points of a meeting, the recorder should take full notes to ensure that nothing has been missed. It is very helpful if copies of reports or other material to be presented at the meeting can be obtained beforehand.

Whether minutes are written up in a formal or informal format, care should be taken to ensure clarity and accessibility. The following style points may be used as general guidelines.

1. Minutes may be either single- or double-spaced. Good-sized margins should be provided when singlespacing minutes.
2. Pages should be numbered consecutively.
3. The substance of the minutes should be presented in a direct manner. The object is to relate what was discussed, what was decided, and what was left undecided as clearly as possible.

If the minutes are long and complex, various devices such as headings, subheadings, paragraph headings, and underscoring may be used. Paragraphs or sections may be numbered according to the numbered items on an agenda. Short meetings involving small groups or limited subjects lend themselves to a concise treatment similar to an outline. It is more common today, however, for minutes to be written in narrative form. In the latter case the person preparing the minutes must be especially careful that summarized information is complete enough to convey what transpired. Above all, it is important that the significant points of a meeting stand out and can be easily located.

Minutes should always be written in objective language. All personal opinions and biases should be excluded.

Index

Various kinds of meetings will require an index of important subjects discussed and actions taken. The index is kept in the form of a card index, with one subject to a card. References are listed chronologically and give the page number of the appropriate minutes.

Agenda

An agenda lists all the specific procedures to be covered at a meeting. The agenda may be formal, including such items as "Reading the minutes of the previous meeting" and "Adjournment." Or it may simply be an informal list of general topics to be discussed.

When preparing an agenda, you must ask every person invited to the meeting if he or she has something to be included. All items should be numbered and double- or triple-spaced to leave room for notes.

PAPERS AND REPORTS

Planning and Research

A paper or report may be undertaken as a school assignment, a job assignment, a professional opportunity (giving a paper or publishing an article), or for other reasons.

At times, a very specific topic is assigned to you. At other times, you may choose any subject that interests you. Often, you are asked to look into a general subject area and choose a specific topic within it.

Certain techniques will be useful to you in preparing papers on any subject. These techniques can be applied to most subjects and will be suitable for a wide variety of source materials.

Basic Research Procedures

There is a great deal of work to be done before you begin to write. A good way to begin is to formulate a tentative title (which may or may not be the final title of your paper). The tentative theme may be too broad or too narrow. It may be a topic that you do not have the facilities to research. The title is merely a first statement of the general area of your research.

By definition, all research papers are based on some kind of data. All research papers also require that the writer collect, organize, present, and evaluate the data. Some papers rely very heavily on other people's evaluations. Other papers rely more heavily on the writer's own evaluations. In either case, it is not enough simply to reproduce sources.

The Source Materials

Before you commit yourself to a topic, consider the materials you will need: books, magazine articles, newspaper clippings, maps, recordings, sheet music, statistics, informants, etc. Begin to examine the library and make preliminary inquiries into other sources. Can you find what you need? If not, you will have to look farther afield, or you may have to restate your topic.

Breaking Down the Topic

At this point, make some preliminary notes for an outline. The outline notes may be revised, expanded, or totally reorganized once your research is under way. The data you encounter may not be what you expect to find, or it may set you thinking in a different line of reasoning. But you need some notes to start you off. Take one topic as an example:

What will the world's population be in the year 2000?
   Reasons for asking the question
   Predictions:
      On what basis are they made?
      Do experts agree?

Are there areas of general agreement?
Are there areas of major disagreement?
The unpredictable:
What events could alter predictions?
How likely are those events?
Have events altered past predictions?
Your own evaluations based on the source materials.

As you begin to read, you may want to shift your outline to stress a particular aspect of the topic:

Shifts in the ratio of older people
Relation of population growth to earth's resources
Differences in population trends in developed and developing nations

Planning the Work

It is best to begin by reading a general book or article about your topic. You may be fortunate enough to find an article that provides a good overall picture of the subject.

Once you have found a background source, further research may be structured in several ways. Different aspects of a topic may be studied one after another. More general material may be examined before more specific material. Material that is easier to understand may be examined before more difficult material, or data may be examined at random.

Practical considerations often impose a sequence of study. For example, research that requires travel must be planned for carefully. Sometimes it is necessary to wait for a reserved book or an inter-library loan. Time must be allotted realistically. Some extra time should always be allowed for the unexpected.

Taking Notes

As you work, you will need to keep notes of what you learn. It is advisable to equip yourself with two kinds of index cards (either two sizes or two colors). One set of cards will be used to record your sources. Each card will represent a different source. The second set of cards will be used to take notes of specific information gained from a source. These cards will contain much of the substance of your paper. They will record quotes, opinions, analyses, and other data. They may also contain your own opinions of what you encounter.

In addition to the cards, some of your "notes" may be photocopies of library materials that you will need for reference. Copying machines help you duplicate charts, tables, statistics, as well as long quotations that you may want to use or consult.

Source Cards

An index card should be made out for every source you consult. You may not quote every book and article, or even refer to each specifically, but you will probably want to include each in your bibliography.

Source cards will provide the data for bibliographies and footnotes. You can record your own general comments about each source on the card. And, because you have the full data on the source card, you will not need to repeat the full information on each information card.

For a *book,* include the following:

- author's full name
- full title and subtitle
- publisher
- city of publication
- most recent copyright date
- edition (if there are several)
- editor, translator, or reviser (if any)
- number of pages

Most of this information will be found on the title page and the reverse of the title page (copyright page). Use the information as you find it. Use the publisher's name as it appears on that book. Indicate only the first city listed.

For a *magazine* or *newspaper article,* include:

- name of author (if any)
- name of magazine or newspaper
- volume and issue numbers
- the pages on which the article is found
- title of the article
- the date

Also keep cards for maps, sketches, works of art, recordings, filmstrips, and any other material you use.

Make notes of the relevant numbers, the location (such as "city hall"), title (if any), and anything else that would enable you or someone else to find that same item again. Mark the source of any material you photocopy.

Information Cards

Most of your notes will record information or opinions you encounter. You may find yourself making a considerable number of information cards from one source and very few cards from another. Some notes will record specific statements, others will summarize ideas. Still others will contain brief quotations (*in quotation marks*). All cards should show the author's name and the page number (or numbers) from which the data was taken. If you are using more than one book or article by the same author, the title may substitute for the author's name. You have the full information for all these sources on your source cards.

Much of what you learned in your research will not be taken in notes. You will be forming ideas about the topic and the manner in which you intend to pursue it. Before you reach the end of your reseach, you should be able to prepare an outline that will show the final plan of the paper you will write.

Outlines

A substantial paper or report needs a good outline. A well-written paper is based on a well-balanced outline. In the finished product, the framework may be obvious or hidden, but it must be there.

A good outline has a structure of major divisions and subdivisions.

I. Roman numerals (**I, II, III**, etc.) mark off the major divisions of ideas in the paper.

   A. Capital letters (**A, B, C**, etc.) are used to subdivide ideas within each Roman numeral group.

      1. Arabic numerals (**1, 2, 3**, etc.) subdivide the ideas within each capital letter group.

         a. Lower-case letters (**a, b, c**, etc.) form the subgroups within the arabic numeral divisions.

It is not necessary to subdivide each topic. No topic, however, should have an A subhead without also having a B subhead. Similarly, if there is a **1**, there must be a **2**; if there is an **a**, there must be a **b**. In other words, there should be at least two subdivisions within a category.

The subdivisions within an outline should be balanced. All **I** topics should be as important as **II** and **III** topics. Within each further division, there should also be balance.

Let us examine some possible outlines for the subject "What will the world's population be in the year 2000?" Note that in each example below, the title and the basic point of the outline in the paragraph following the title have been restated to suit the particular subject eventually chosen.

Outline 1

PLANNING FOR AN OLDER POPULATION

All evidence indicates that the proportion of old people to young people in society is increasing. The shift will require new planning for the future.

I. Evidence of the shift
    A. The declining birthrate
    B. The changing death rate
    C. Population profiles for the future
        1. Profiles based on current rates
        2. Profiles based on various predictions for the future
            a. same birthrate, lower death rate
            b. lower birthrate, same death rate
            c. lower birth and death rates

II. Implications of the population shift
    A. For work and retirement patterns
        1. Current patterns
        2. Prospective patterns
    B. For government planning
        1. Government income
        2. Government services
        3. Need for public institutions
    C. For people planning careers
    D. For industries

III. Planning for the future
    A. Fitting current data into planning schemes
    B. Monitoring future changes

IV. Steps to begin to take now

Outline 1 was written in phrases. The same outline can be written out in full sentences. It is often advisable to do so. Here, for example, is a fuller version of section I.

Outline 2

PLANNING FOR AN OLDER POPULATION

All evidence indicates that the proportion of old people to young people in society is increasing. The shift will require new planning for the future.

I. Evidence of the shift in the ratio of older people in the population is available in our present statistics.
   A. The birthrate is declining. Fewer children are born to the average woman.
   B. The death rate is decreasing. More people are reaching a greater age.
   C. From present statistics we can provide a profile of future population ratios. All profiles will suggest an older population.
      1. We can project the profiles by assuming the same birthrate and a lower death rate.
      2. We can assume a lower birthrate and the same death rate.
      3. We can assume both lower birth and death rates based on current trends.

The outline in sentence form is much clearer than the phrasal outline. A sentence outline can often help to clarify thinking about a subject. It will reveal the strengths and weaknesses of the structure better than a phrasal outline will.

Below is an example of another outline (and a different title) based on similar subject matter.

Outline 3

IS THE WORLD'S POPULATION OUTGROWING ITS RESOURCES?

The potential for population growth seems to be infinite. The world's population is doubling in shorter periods of time. The potential for developing the world's resources seems to be finite. Some people claim that we are rapidly approaching our population limits. Others claim that the crisis will not occur.

I. A historical look reveals the accelerating rate of population growth, food production, and energy growth and consumption.
   A. Patterns and rates of population growth have varied in specific periods of the past.
   B. Food production has increased in the past, but not always in step with population growth.
   C. Our need for energy has increased and our sources for energy have decreased.
II. Experts do not agree on the prospects for the future.
   A. Pessimists argue that we are overpopulating the world and cannot forever expect to provide the resources for the people.
      1. They project growth charts that indicate ever greater numbers of people.

2. They cite statistics that indicate limits to our capacity to feed people.
3. They indicate that we are demanding more and more energy and are unable to continue to provide energy in the amount required for an unlimited time.

B. Optimists argue that although there is a theoretical limit to the number of people the world can support, we are not in danger of reaching that limit.
   1. They cite evidence of a leveling-off of population growth—with a possible zero population growth at some time in the future.
   2. They believe that we have not tapped all our food-production facilities and that we have the capacity to provide far more food than we now provide.
   3. They believe that there are new sources of energy that can provide us with an infinite energy supply.

C. There are areas of general agreement among virtually all experts.
   1. It is theoretically possible to overpopulate the world.
   2. Present food-growing techniques will not serve a greatly increased population.
   3. Present energy technology cannot serve our future needs.

III. Whether you believe the optimists or the pessimists, prospects for the future are most hopeful if the rate of population growth slows and the resource potential is expanded.

   A. Several charts are provided to indicate possible future population patterns.

   B. Various new food-producing systems have been successful or unsuccessful. Reasons are examined.

   C. It is too early to evaluate new sources of energy.

Outline 3 differs from Outline 2 in many respects. Outline 3 is subdivided to the same extent as Outline 2, and the items in Outline 3 are balanced to an unusual degree.

An outline will take various shapes depending on the nature of the data and the way the writer assembles the data. By the time the outline is prepared, the writer should know that the data is available. Sometimes the outline will reveal the need for further data in a particular area.

Relation of Information Cards to Outline

Each writer has a distinct style of relating the information cards to the outline. Some people prepare the outline itself by arranging the cards to create a pattern. Other people develop a mental image of an outline as the research progresses. Then they arrange the cards to suit the outline.

Whatever system is used, at some point the cards will have to be organized to fit the outline. It is advisable to make notes of the subtopic on an upper corner of each card.

A finished paper should never read like an assortment of cards. The data on the cards will be used indirectly in some instances and directly in other instances. Sometimes a card will be no more than a way of reminding you to include an idea. Some cards may be irrelevant to the final topic. The notes may have been made before a final outline was drafted. Do not hesitate to eliminate irrelevant information. It is important for a writer to develop a sense of what is relevant and what is not.

Formats

Style Points

A clean and inviting appearance is one of the most important considerations when putting a piece of writing into final form, whether you are composing an original paper based on your own research or organizing and styling a report based on another person's work. All job applicants know the importance of first impressions and hence the need to present a neat appearance when first meeting a prospective employer. Similarly, a cleanly typed and styled paper will encourage a reader to investigate it.

What will the final piece look like? Papers and reports can be written in either a formal or informal format. A formal paper, as we shall see, has a complex structure. An informal paper, on the other hand, may be comprised of only a short text with a title. At its simplest it may take the form of a business letter. But regardless of the format used, the following stylistic points should be observed.

1. All papers and reports need a cover or title page giving the title, the name of the writer, the date, and the name of the class or organization to which the project is being submitted.
2. All pages should be numbered in the same position, either centered at the top or on the upper-right corner.
3. All margins should be uniform. And they should not be skimpy.
4. Any charts, graphs, or similar material should be numbered. A standard style for the title and legend of figures should be maintained.
5. The paper or report should be double-spaced. Any quotation of five lines or more should be single-spaced and indented. Quotation marks should not be used for these. Legends may also be single-spaced.
6. Most papers and reports are typed on standard 8½" by 11" white paper. Certain organizations or kinds of projects require the use of preruled or otherwise nonstandard paper. In any case an original copy should always be typed on high-quality paper.

Organization is the second important consideration when planning the final format of a paper or report. A good appearance will encourage someone to begin reading your work, but only clarity of presentation and substance will get that person to read the piece through to the end and to consider it seriously.

Headings

The first decision you must make is whether a paper or report will benefit from the use of headings. A relatively brief or uncomplicated paper will usually require no headings. If well-planned, the framework should be apparent because the finished work has a logical and natural sequence of thought. A long or complicated paper, however, usually requires headings to distinguish among many topics and subtopics. If you are writing a paper or report from an outline, the outline itself will provide the headings and subheadings. If you are working from raw data or a rough outline, you will have to formulate headings. Headings should be brief and informative. Use a single word or a phrase instead of a complete sentence.

Let's say you are writing a paper titled "Planning for an Older Population." If you were working from Outline 1, the paper might have the following headings:

EVIDENCE OF THE SHIFT TO AN OLDER POPULATION
The Declining Birthrate
The Changing Death Rate

IMPLICATIONS OF THE POPULATION SHIFT
For Work and Retirement Patterns
Current patterns
Prospective patterns

> For Government Planning
> Government income
> Government services

Note that the gradation in importance of the headings is conveyed by the different styles in which they are printed. Each category of heading should be treated identically. If the first main heading is typed in capital letters and underlined, all successive main headings should be typed in capital letters and underlined.

The Formal Report

A formal paper or report is made up of different parts, each having a distinct purpose. (Many organizations have a preferred format; if so this will simplify your task.) What follows is the general format of a formal report; it is intended only as a guide and its various sections are adaptable to the needs of a specific project. However, a formal report always includes sections 1, 4, and 5.

1. Title Page and/or Cover
2. Introduction/Preface or Letter of Transmittal
3. Abstract or Summary
4. Table of Contents
   List of Tables and Illustrations
5. Text
   a. Introduction
   b. Discussion
   c. Conclusions and/or Recommendations
6. Appendix

7. Bibliography
8. Index

Title Page. This page contains the title of the paper, the name of the writer (and his or her position, if applicable), the name and address of the department or company (if the paper is written as a job assignment) or the name of the class (if the paper is written as a school project), and the date.

Cover. An informal paper often dispenses with a full title page and instead has a cover giving the title, the writer's name, and sometimes the name of the company or class to which it is submitted. A formal paper may have both a title page and a cover.

Introduction/Preface or Letter of Transmittal. An introduction or preface is a short statement of the subject, purpose, and scope of the paper along with any necessary information about its writer or background about its preparation. A letter of transmittal is more formal than, and is used in place of, an introduction. It is typed on regular business letterhead. In addition to giving some or all of the information contained in an introduction, it is directed specifically to the authorization or request for the paper.

Any acknowledgments, as of contributors, assistants, or sources that are not mentioned elsewhere, should appear in a separate paragraph at the end of the introduction or letter of transmittal.

Abstract or Summary. This is a brief synopsis, normally in one or two paragraphs, of the problem dealt with in the paper, the methodology used in examining it, and the conclusions reached. Once found almost exclusively in technical studies, the abstract is now widely used in academic and business papers. Its condensed form makes it useful in research and as accessible reference material; hence it has become one of the most important parts of a formal paper or report.

Table of Contents. This lists the titles of the chapters or principal sections of the paper (and their numbers, if any are used), the subheadings or subtopics within each chapter or section, the appendix, bibliography, and index, and the page number on which each begins. Since the actual text of any paper always begins on page 1, all pages preceding the text (including the table of contents) are numbered in Roman numerals and should be so listed in the contents table if you choose to include them. Everything listed in the table of contents should be entered in the exact order in which it appears in the finished work.

The heading of the page, always centered, is *Contents* (*Table of* is now considered extraneous). The table itself begins an inch or two below the heading and is set up in outline form. Chapters, sections, etc., are placed on the left side of the page and page numbers on the right. You may use a string of periods as a leader to connect the left-hand entry to the page number if you wish. In addition, many people use the subheadings *Chapter* and *Page* on top of the left- and right-hand columns respectively.

List of Tables and Illustrations. Many papers make extensive use of tables and illustrations (all illustrations are individually referred to in text as *figures*).

These lists follow the table of contents and have the headings *Tables* and *Illustrations*. If the contents page is set with column subheadings, these lists should conform to style, using *Table* and *Figure* on the left and *Page* on the right.

Text.   The text of a paper or report should be a logically organized and clearly written presentation. An introduction states the purpose and scope of the project, the methodology used, any pertinent background information, and a brief statement of the conclusions drawn. The discussion is a detailed study of the subject, presented as briefly and succinctly as possible. The final section of the text presents a full explanation of the conclusions and/or recommendations produced by the study.

Appendix.   All supplementary materials, such as maps, charts, or graphs, that provide background to or amplification of the topic are listed in the appendix. If there are two or more appendixes, they should be distinguished by letters (capitals) or numbers (Arabic or Roman, though the latter should be used only if they are not used to refer to chapters or sections). A glossary of pertinent terms or list of abbreviations may be placed in the appendix or in a separate section immediately following.

Bibliography.   A paper or report that makes use of material from outside sources (including such things as unpublished articles or reports and speeches) requires a bibliography citing those sources (see page 217).

Index.   An index is used primarily in a long and involved work. It lists in alphabetical order all the main topics covered in the paper or report and can usually be put together by rearranging the table of contents. Certain works, however, require a detailed index that goes beyond the contents page listings and can only be drawn from the text itself. This can be a difficult task and there is a specific method to follow (see page 219).

Writing the Paper

It is not necessary to be a great writer to produce a good paper or report. It is necessary to have a good grasp of the major ideas, good information, and a good outline. By the time you are ready to write, you should be familiar with any new words or terms used in the field, and you should be capable of explaining them.

The most difficult part to write is the first paragraph. It should set the stage for what follows. A first paragraph may raise an interesting question that you will answer or attempt to answer later in the paper. It may, instead, propose an idea that will be examined. It may argue a cause, state a conclusion, or do any of a number of other things. At times, a first paragraph may begin with a quotation that will serve as a theme for agreement or disagreement. Above all, the first paragraph should be interesting and should be related to the rest of the paper.

Keep your writing as simple as possible. Use unusual long words when they are the most appropriate words, but do not try to introduce learned words just to sound learned. If the subject you are dealing with has its own vocabulary, do use the appropriate vocabulary. Try to avoid sentences that must be read and reread to arrive at their meaning. Often such sentences can be broken down to their components and rewritten with greater clarity.

There should be a logical flow from sentence to sentence and paragraph to paragraph. One idea will flow into the next, and your writing will be persuasive. Often when a flow of ideas is lacking, it is because the writer has not absorbed the material well and is simply recording one note after another.

A logic should also exist from section to section of a work. Transition sentences or paragraphs prepare the way for the introduction of new subject matter.

Many people believe that clear writing is related to clear thinking. If you are having a great deal of trouble putting your thoughts into writing, re-examine your thinking. Are you confident of your ideas and your data? Can other conclusions be drawn from your work? If so, how will you deal with them? If you are not confident of your material, do you have enough time to do some more research? If not, can you redefine and limit your topic to material with which you are comfortable?

The preparation of any written work offers an opportunity for the writer to examine new topics, learn new research procedures, and sharpen writing skills. Some papers may be more successful than others, but over the years a person should gain confidence and ability in preparing them.

Preparing Footnotes

Footnotes are an important element in any paper or report because they can convey many kinds of information. They must, however, be used judiciously; an absence of any or an overabundance can ruin the finished work. Footnotes are used for specific purposes:

1. To give the source of quotations, charts, tables, graphs, statistics that you copy as found.
2. To give the source of ideas, arguments, facts, or other data that you present in your own words or diagrams.
3. To give the source of something that is not gleaned from general research.
4. To substantiate your own arguments.
5. To offer comments that are not part of the main idea.

Reference footnotes have a particular style. They begin with a number (typed half space above the line) and are followed by the remaining data. The first reference to a book or article is usually given in full. Further references are given in short form. Below are some examples of footnotes:

First Mention of a Book

[1]John Wain, *Samuel Johnson* (New York: The Viking Press, 1974), p. 183.

Further references to the same book:

[2]Wain, p. 187.

Two Books by Same Author(s)

[3]Carl Bernstein and Bob Woodward, *All the President's Men* (New York: Simon and Schuster, 1974), p. 71.

Further references:

[4]Bernstein and Woodward, *President's Men*, p. 92.

[5]Bob Woodward and Carl Bernstein, *The Final Days* (New York: Simon and Schuster, 1976), p. 77.

Further references:

[6]Woodward and Bernstein, *Final Days*, p. 283.

(Note that even though the authors have listed their names in reverse order on the second book, it is advisable to repeat the title in further references to avoid confusion.)

Book With an Editor, but no Author

[7]Fred L. Israel, ed., *1897 Sears Roebuck Catalog* (New York: Chelsea House, 1968), p. 149.

Article in an Anthology

[8]John T. Hitchcock, "Fieldwork in Ghurka Country," in *Being an Anthropologist,* ed. George D. Spindler (New York: Holt, Rinehart and Winston, 1970), pp. 164–165.

Further references:

[9]Hitchcock, p. 173.

Signed Magazine Article

[10]Edwin S. Dethlefsen and Kenneth Jensen, "Social

Commentary from the Cemetery," *Natural History,* June–July 1977, p. 34.

Further references:

[11]Dethlefsen and Jensen, p. 37.

Unsigned Magazine Article

[12]"Estrogen Therapy: The Dangerous Road to Shangri-La," *Consumer Reports,* Nov. 1976, p. 642.

Further references:

[13]"Estrogen Therapy," p. 644.

Signed Encyclopedia Article

[14]Philip James, "Orchestration," *Encyclopedia International,* 1972, Vol. 13, pp. 464–466.

Famous Play

[15]*Much Ado about Nothing,* III, iii, 53–55.

The styles of footnotes used to add commentary or asides may vary. One example would be:

[16]The *Oxford English Dictionary* gives an obsolete meaning for *population* as "devastation, laying waste." Many who fear the effects of overpopulation might tend to support this definition.

(Note: the *Oxford English Dictionary* is a standard general reference. Unlike other references cited, it would not normally appear in a bibliography.)

Footnotes should be typed single-space at the bottom of the page or they can be listed at the end of each section or at the end of the text itself. If placed on the page, footnotes should be typed single-space with a double space between them if there are two or more.

Notes are separated from the text by a short line. You must be careful when typing to leave enough room at the bottom to fit in all the footnotes on the page. Notes placed at the end of a section have the centered heading "Footnotes" or simply "Notes." If all the notes are placed at the end of the text you will need to provide the appropriate chapter or section headings.

The works listed in the footnotes, as well as other works that might not be quoted directly, are listed in the bibliography.

Preparing a Bibliography

Strictly speaking, a bibliography is a list of books or printed articles, but it may also include material other than printed matter (interviews, graphic works, filmstrips, etc.).

Items in a bibliography follow a particular format. Note that the format is *not* the same as the format for footnotes.

1. *Author's name* is given last name first. If there is more than one author, all the authors after the first are listed first name first.

   All books by one author are listed before the books in which that author collaborated with another.

   A period follows the author's name.

2. *Full titles are given and underlined* if they are titles of books. Titles of stories, poems, and articles are given in quotation marks. A period follows the title.

3. City of publication, followed by a colon and the

publisher (as shown on the book used) are given, followed by the copyright date.

4. For articles, stories, and poems, the pages on which they appear are given.

What do you list in a bibliography? Certainly, you list all books or articles that have been footnoted. Often you list other books or articles that proved useful as general background but not as a source of specific footnotes. Do not list books that were consulted but did not prove helpful.

Sample Bibliography

BIBLIOGRAPHY

Carson, Rachel. *The Sea Around Us*. New York: The New American Library, 1961.

——. *Silent Spring*. Boston: Houghton Mifflin Company, 1962.

Hamilton, Roger. "Can We Harness the Wind?" *National Geographic,* December, 1975.

Hitchcock, John T., "Fieldwork in Ghurka Country." In *Being an Anthropologist,* ed. George D. Spindler. New York: Holt, Rinehart and Winston, 1970, pp. 164—193.

Kahn, Herman. *Thinking about the Unthinkable*. New York: Horizon Press, 1962.

—— and Anthony J. Wiener. *The Year 2000*. New York: Macmillan Company, 1967.

Ternes, Alan, ed. *Ants, Indians, and Little Dinosaurs*. New York: Charles Scribner's Sons, 1975.

Note: If you list two books by one writer, the name may be replaced by a dash for the second reference.

Preparing An Index

An index is a list of all significant topics covered in a paper, report, book, article, etc. It is made from the page proofs of a printed work or the final copy of a typed work to ensure that all page numbers are final. The following procedure is used in compiling an index.

Working with the text, underline all items to be indexed; these include chapter or section headings and subheadings, important ideas and theories, and the names of events, places, people, things, etc.

The second step is to transfer the information to 3″ by 5″ cards. Write the subject on the top left, followed by a comma and the appropriate page number or numbers. Use a separate card for each item, including cross-references.

Next arrange the cards alphabetically by subject. During this step you should remove all insignificant items. An overlong index containing trivial entries will be of little use to the reader.

Finally, type the entries double-spaced in a list in either a single- or double-column format. The latter style is preferable and the entries in most indexes should be brief enough to accommodate it.

A number of points should be kept in mind. Entries should be as brief and specific as possible, usually a single word or a phrase. Always index according to the most important word in a phrase.

address to, forms of, 162–174

Avoid if possible a string of page references following a single entry. In such a situation you will usually be able to develop subentries from the text to indicate what aspect of the entry is dealt with at each reference.

For cross-references use the words "See" or "See also." The former is a straight cross-reference and does not have page numbers, which are always entered at the primary index entry. Page numbers are entered when "See also" is used since the cross-reference is to additional information at another entry.

PROOFREADING

At one time or another everyone has done some simple proofreading, such as reading over a letter to see that everything is correct or checking over a list to see that nothing has been omitted. Strict proofreading involves marking corrections in copy with textual symbols and marginal notations. Knowing how to use proofreaders' marks is helpful if you are a student proofing a theme to be typed or an office worker proofing the final copy of a report, financial statement, etc., before or after it is typed or printed by a compositor.

The act of proofreading involves checking a typed or printed piece of copy against the original manuscript. While there is no single preferred method used in proofreading, there are basic guidelines.

1. Take as much time as you need to ensure accuracy. Most copy to be proofread, especially material that

comes from a compositor, has very few mistakes. It is as easy to miss errors in clean copy as it is in dirty copy.

2. Read the copy through to the end once to understand its meaning; then forget about meaning. While some people appreciate suggestions, for example, how wording could be improved, the proofreader's primary responsibility is seeing that everything that is supposed to be in the text is in and that the material is correctly spelled, spaced, etc.

   It is a good idea to read through the copy a number of times, checking for different things on each pass (i.e., spelling and punctuation, spacing and alignment). Read the copy three or four characters at a time, saying each letter, punctuation mark, and word space aloud. Remember that a misplaced comma is as crucial an error as a misspelled word. Complicated material, such as intricate tables and charts, is best proofread by two people, one reading from the original while the other checks the copy.

3. Take nothing for granted. Spelling and punctuation errors get by the proofreader who does not check every single word or mark that he or she is unsure about. Remember that even the original copy can contain spelling errors. Important pieces of copy should receive a second proofreading by another proofreader.

What follows is a chart containing the proofreaders' marks and a sample of marked copy.

Proofreaders' Marks

Instruction	Mark in Margin	Mark in Type
Delete	(del)	the good word
Insert indicated material	good	the ∧ word
Let it stand	(stet)	the good word
Make capital	(cap)	the good word
Make lower case	(lc)	the Word
Set in small capitals	(sc)	See word
Set in italic type	(ital)	The word is word
Set in boldface type	(bf)	the word
Set in roman type	(rom)	the entry word
Set in lightface type	(lf)	the entry word
Transpose	(tr)	the wo/rd good
Close up space	( )	the wo rd
Delete and close up space	(◠)	the wo rd
Spell out	(sp)	(2) words
Insert space	#	the word
period	⊙	This is the word
comma	∧	words, words, words
hyphen	=	word for word test

Instruction	Mark in Margin	Mark in Type
colon	(:)	The following words, skim the words.
semicolon	;	Scan the words skim the words.
apostrophe	∨	Johns words
quotation marks	∨∨	the word word
parentheses	(/)	The word is from the Word in parentheses.
brackets	[/]	He read from the Word the Bible.
en dash	-N-	1964 1972
em dash	-M-	The dictionary how often it is needed, belongs in every home.
Start paragraph	¶	"Where is it?" "It's on the shelf."
Move left	⊏	⊏ the word
Move right	⊐	the word
Align	‖	the word / the word
Wrong font	(wf)	the word
Broken type	X	the word

Sample Copy

It is the proofreader's job to ensure that all
typed or printed material is properly spaced and
aligned and contains grammatical, typographical, or
spelling errors. Mark all corrections in a color that
is clearly distinguished from the copy. Each
correction requires a symbol in the text and a corresponding explanation in the margin next to the line
in which it is found. If there are 2 or more corrections in one line, write them in the margin in the proper order and separate them with a slanting line. Material to be inserted is written in the margin and its
place is indicated by a caret. If you make an
improper correction and these things do happen do
not erase it, put a series of periods below what you
have mistakenly corrected in the text and write stet
which means "Let it stand" in the margin.

Always remember to take your time. The proofreader has
only one goal total accuracy. Never assume or guess that
something is right. Check every word whose spelling you
are unsure of in your copy of The American Heritage Dictionary.

223

THE LIBRARY

The Card Catalog

The card catalog is your best tool for finding books in the library. In some libraries, the card catalog may also help you locate records, filmstrips, microfilms, microfiches, etc. In other libraries, these materials may have their own reference systems. But books will be listed in the card catalog.

What exactly is a card catalog? A card catalog is an index of books, arranged alphabetically in a set of file drawers usually with 3″ x 5″ cards. Each file drawer is usually labeled to show what portion of the alphabet it contains. The cards list the information about the books: author, title, subject or subjects covered in the book. Some cards give cross-references to other cards. A few cards are information cards: they do not direct you to a particular book, but tell you where to find cards for items that may be hard to locate.

No matter where a book is situated in the library, the card will direct you to it. Although the cards are listed alphabetically, the books are not arranged alphabetically on the shelves. Libraries in the United States usually organize their books by one of two systems: the Dewey Decimal System, or the Library of Congress System. Both systems classify books into the major fields of knowledge, and will be explained in the section "Organization of the Library." Thus, mathematics books will be in one section, history books in another, and so on. Within each broad area of knowledge there are subdivisions. While these systems create an orderly arrangement for the library, without the card catalog it would be very difficult for the average individual to find the required books. The card catalog is an efficient way of directing people to the books they want. Cards are added to the catalog for new books as the books are acquired; cards are eliminated for books that are discarded. Material on the cards can help a person decide if that book will be helpful.

Organization of the Cards

The cards in the card catalog are alphabetized word by word. That means that all the cards beginning, for example, with "New" will be placed before the cards beginning with "News" or "Newton." Thus the order will be:

New astronomy theories
New Jersey
New mathematics
New ports
New theories of science
New York
Newark
Newport
News
News gathering
Newton, Isaac
Newtonian physics
Newts

The word-by-word method of alphabetizing differs from the method used by dictionaries. In dictionaries, each word or phrase is alphabetized as if it were written as one word. In a dictionary system, "Newark" would come before "New Jersey" and "New York."

Also, in a card catalog, all abbreviations are listed as if they were spelled out. Thus, "Mt." would be listed as if spelled "mount" and "St." would be listed as if spelled "saint." "Mc" and "M'" would be listed as if spelled "Mac." Articles (a, an, the) are not considered if they appear at the beginning of a title. (*The House of Seven Gables* would be alphabetized at *House*, not at *The*.)

If there are books *by* a person and *about* that same person, all the books *by* that author would be listed before all the books *about* the author.

In situations that are very complicated, an information card in the drawer will often clarify matters. For example, there are many kings named Henry from many countries. There are also people whose last names are Henry. How do you figure out which comes first? An information card will usually explain the order used in the catalog.

What Do the Cards Tell You?

So far, we have investigated how the cards are arranged in the catalog. But the cards are designed to direct you to the books themselves. To find the books, you need to understand what can be learned from the cards.

In the first place, a card in the catalog tells you that the book you want is in the library's collection. The card will not tell you if someone else has the book out on loan, and in many libraries, will not indicate whether the book is at the bindery for repairs. The card will let you know whether the book may be borrowed or must be used in the library, in which case the card is stamped "Reference." In some cases, the most recent edition of a book is a reference book, but an older edition of the same book may be taken out on loan. Then there are usually two cards in the catalog. One is stamped "Reference," the other is not. Or the word "Reference" is inked out on the older card.

Other items that may be learned from a catalog card are: the author's full name, date of birth, date of death, title and subtitle of book, copyright date of the book, number of pages, and publisher. You can learn whether the book has illustrations, a bibliography, an introduction by someone other than the author. Some cards will give the date when a book was first published if the book is a new edition or revision. At the bottom of the card, there are notaions that indicate where other cards may be found in the catalog for that same book. These notations can be helpful if you want to pursue the subject matter in other books.

The most important thing that you can learn from the card is the book's *call number,* which will direct you to the shelf on which the book can be found. The call number may look like this: 828.609 (B) if the book is classified by the Dewey Decimal System, or like this: PR3533.w33 if the book is classified by the Library of Congress system. Some books may have no call number. Works of fiction—especially contemporary fiction—are often arranged by author's last name in a separate fiction section in a library. Some catalog cards may have *Fic.* or *F.* in the corner where one would normally find the call number. Other libraries place nothing at all on the fiction cards.

Biographies may be treated as a separate category in some libraries. The call number on a biography book may simply be a *B* (for biography) followed by the first initial of the last name of the person about whom the book is written. Thus, a biography *about* Sigmund Freud would have B-F where the call number would normally appear. A biography *by* Sigmund Freud *about* Woodrow Wilson would have B-W for the call number.

Before we pursue the question of library organization, let us consider some sample catalog cards.

Author Cards

Librarians consider the author card to be the basic catalog card. Most books have authors. Sometimes the author is one individual. Sometimes several people, a committee, foundation, magazine, or even the U.S. Government may be the "author" of a book.

The author card lists the author's name, last name first. On the line below, it lists the title of the book. If there are ten books in the library by one author, there will be ten author cards, one for each book. Those cards will be listed alphabetically by their titles.

For example, if you wanted to find books written by Herman Kahn, you would look up "Kahn, Herman" and find:

```
Kahn, Herman
    Thinking about the unthinkable.  Horizon
Press [c1962]  254 p.




                Includes bibliographical references.


1. Atomic warfare             2. U.S.--For. rel.
I Title
```

After that card, you might find:

```
Kahn, Herman   1922-                    301.2-K

    The year 2000; a framework for speculation
on the next thirty-three years by Herman Kahn
and Anthony J. Wiener, with contributions
from other staff members of the Hudson Institute.
Introd. by Daniel Bell.  New York, Macmillan
(c1967), 431 p. illus.



I. Twentieth century    Forecasts 1. Hudson
Institute   II. Title
```

The first book, *Thinking About the Unthinkable,* was written in 1962 by Herman Kahn. It has 254 pages and bibliographical references. Other catalog cards may be found at: Atomic warfare, U.S.-Foreign relations, and *Thinking About the Unthinkable.*

Most important of all, the card tells you that the book will be found on the shelf with other books having the number 355K. (The K is for Kahn).

The second book by Herman Kahn has a different number: 301.2–K. It falls into a different subject area. It was written by Herman Kahn and other people. Its copyright date is 1967. The book has 431 pages and is illustrated. Other catalog cards for the same book may be found at: Twentieth century, forecasts, Hudson Institute, and (*The*) *Year 2000.*

Some authors do not write under their own names. The library may list the book at the pseudonym or at the real name. The card catalog will clarify the name and the spelling that the library uses.

```
Twain, Mark

    see

Clemens, Samuel Langhorne
```

All the catalog cards for Mark Twain will be found under "Clemens." And you will find, when you look at the Clemens cards, that not all the fiction by Mark Twain is to be found in the fiction section. Some will be found in the American Literature section. The call number will direct you to the correct section.

Not all writers who use pseudonyms are listed at their real names. When you look up an author, look under the name that you are familiar with. The card catalog will inform you whether the author is listed by his or her pseudonym or real name.

The United States government and its branches may be the "author" of a book. If you try to look up "Library of Congress" in the card catalog, a cross-reference card will tell you to look under "U.S. Library of Congress." There you will find books with "U.S. Library of Congress" as the official author. Following all the author cards, you will find books *about* the Library of Congress. Some of the books about the Library of Congress may have been compiled by the U.S. Library of Congress staff. Others may have been written by individuals.

Title Cards

Suppose that you know the title of a book, but don't know who wrote it. The card catalog can help you find it. Titles are also listed in the card catalog in alphabetical order.

The title card gives the title above the author's name. The title is usually typed in. Then the author's name is given, and the title is repeated again. A title card is really the basic author card with the title shown at the top.

If you wanted to find a book named *My Antonia,* you would look under *My.*

```
    My Antonia
Cather, Willa Sibert
    My Antonia.  Houghton Mifflin Co.
Boston.      371 p.
```

There is no call number on this card because it is a work of fiction and will be found in the fiction section under Cather.

Sometimes several short novels are bound into one volume. The volume may have the title of one of the short novels. How do you find the other short novels? Try this card catalog. For example, if you wanted to find *Neighbour Rosicky,* look up *Neighbour:*

```
    Neighbour Rosicky
Cather, Willa Sibert
    Neighbour Rosicky (In Obscure destinies.)
```

The short novel *Neighbour Rosicky* may be found in the volume *Obscure Destinies*. Although the card catalog may help you find short novels, it will usually *not* help you find short stories, poems, plays, and essays. To find these you need reference books. (See the next section, "Basic Reference Materials.")

The main thing to remember when looking for a title card is to ignore the article at the beginning of the title. Look for *A Tale of Two Cities* at "Tale," not at "A." Look for *The Uses of Enchantment* at "Uses" not at "The."

Suppose you are not sure if the name by which you know a book is an author's name or the title. For example, if you wanted to find *The Guinness Book of World Records,* look it up under *Guinness.*

```
                              Reference
Guinness book of world records. Sterling
   Pub. Co. 19--   illus. ports

   Title varies: The Guinness book of

superlatives.


1. Curiosities.   (1) Title: The Guinness
book of superlatives
```

The authors' names are omitted from this card, but a card for an older edition reveals that the authors were Norris McWhirter and Ross McWhirter.

Some books—such as reference books—have no official author, since they are compiled by groups of people. When they are published, these books can be located by their titles.

Subject Cards

Most researchers find that the subject cards are the most useful cards in the catalog. Often there are some cards that refer you to books that cover the broad subject and other cards that refer to books on subdivisions of the subject. There may also be an information card that leads you to related topics.

Suppose that you are doing some research on costumes. Perhaps you must design and make costumes for a play that takes place in eighteenth-century England. You look up the subject COSTUME in the card catalog. Note that the subject card is the basic author card with the subject printed (or typed) in capitals at the top of the card.

```
COSTUME

Evans, Mary    1890-        391-E
   Costume through the ages.  Philadelphia,
Lippincott (c 1950)  360 p. illus. ports.



   "Revised edition."
   Includes bibliographies.


1. Costume    2. Costume - Hist.    I Title
```

The first book you see is *Costume Through the Ages* by Mary Evans. It has illustrations and portraits, and it is a revised edition. That suggests that it was sufficiently interesting to bring out a revised edition. It also has bibliographies. But since the copyright date is 1950, any books listed in the bibliographies will have been printed before 1950.

Other books are listed under the general subject COSTUME. There is also a cross-reference card:

```
COSTUME

    see also

CHURCH VESTMENTS
CLOTHING AND DRESS
FASHION
UNIFORMS
```

These other subjects may or may not be useful in your research. You make a note of the subjects that may help.

After the general subject COSTUME are books on particular aspects of the general subject. For example:

COSTUME—GREAT BRITAIN

COSTUME, THEATRICAL

Both of these subcategories will be helpful in the particular research you are doing, and you note the books listed under each one.

For example, this card may appear:

```
COSTUME, THEATRICAL

    Voland, Virginia              792.42-V
      Designing women; the art and practice of
    theatrical costume design.  Garden City,
    Doubleday (c 1966) 197 p.
```

The book seems to be one that may help you actually make the costumes once you have decided what
the costumes are to look like. You make a note of it.

The card catalog can lead you to books, but it cannot help you decide if the books are what you need. To
know if a book is useful, you must examine it.

Organization of the Library

Today there are two organizational systems that are
widely used in the United States: the Dewey Decimal
System and the Library of Congress System. When
you enter a library see if the books have Dewey Decimal System call numbers (e.g. 792.42) or Library of
Congress call numbers (e.g. PN 1993.5). Note that the
Dewey Decimal System call numbers begin with
Arabic numerals. The Library of Congress call numbers begin with letters.

The call numbers stand for certain categories. The
categories in the Dewey Decimal System differ from
the categories in the Library of Congress system.

Dewey Decimal System

000	Generalities—bibliographies, encyclopedias, libraries, etc.
100	Philosophy and related disciplines
200	Religion
300	Social science—statistics, political science, economics, law, education, etc.
400	Language—linguistics, other languages
500	Pure sciences—mathematics, astronomy, physics, chemistry, earth science, biological science, botany, zoology, etc.
600	Technology—medicine, engineering, agriculture, domestic science, business, etc.
700	The arts—architecture, sculpture, drawing, painting, photography, music, recreational arts
800	Literature and rhetoric—American and English literature, literature from other languages
900	General geography, history, etc.

Each category is subdivided further (401, 426, 492, etc.) and decimal numbers may be added to make further distinctions (426.12, 792.42, etc.). On the shelf, all the books are arranged in numerical order. Books without the decimal are arranged before books with the decimal (792, 792.12, 792.42, etc.)

Library of Congress System

A	General works
B	Philosophy and religion
C	History and auxiliary sciences

D	History and topography (except America)
E & F	America
G	Geography and anthropology
H	Social sciences
J	Political sciences
K	Law
L	Education
M	Music
N	Fine arts
P	Language and literature
Q	Science
R	Medicine
S	Agriculture
T	Technology
U	Military science
V	Naval science
Z	Bibliography and library science

Note that the letters I, O, W, X, and Y are not included. If further categories become necessary, they may some day be used.

Categories in the Library of Congress System are further subdivided with a second letter, then a numeral of one to four digits, then a decimal followed by a numeral or a letter and a numeral. Sometimes there is a further subdivision of categories introduced by a second decimal.

On the shelf, books are arranged alphabetically by letter categories (P, PN, PS, etc.). Within each of the letter categories, books are arranged in numerical order from 1 to 9999 (PN1, PN86, PN1993, PN1993.5, PN1994, PN6110, etc.)

Library Reference Sources

After you have searched through the card catalog, you have not yet exhausted the resources of the library. Most libraries have reference sections—separate rooms or areas—containing books that are often consulted as references. Some items may very clearly be reference books: encyclopedias, dictionaries, almanacs, atlases, etc. Other items may not fit as obviously into the category of reference books: anthologies, books of documents, etc. In addition, some valuable reference material may be found not in the reference section but in the general collection.

There are two kinds of library reference sources. One kind supplies the required information—you look in the book and find what you want to know. The other kind directs you to the required information in another book, magazine, newspaper, etc. Both kinds are needed for most reference projects. Read the introductions to the reference books carefully. Each book organizes material in its own way. Each has its own abbreviations and cross-references.

Indexes to Newspapers and Periodicals

An index is a guide to direct you to material on a subject or by an author. Using an index involves two processes. The first is finding out whether and where an article has been published. The second process is sometimes more difficult—finding a copy of the required newspaper or magazine. Large libraries may have bound volumes of periodicals and microfilm or microfiche copies of newspapers.

Most magazines have their own yearly indexes. Once a year, they prepare an alphabetical list of the articles that have appeared over that year.

Readers' Guide to Periodical Literature directs you to articles in the most widely read magazines in the United States. Regular supplements are available to bring you up to date. *Access* directs you to some periodicals not indexed in *Readers' Guide*. There are also indexes to direct you to more specialized journals in particular fields. A short list of examples includes:

> *Agricultural Index*
> *Applied Science and Technology Index*
> *Art Index*
> *Business Periodicals Index*
> *Cumulative Book Index*
> *Education Index*
> *Humanities Index*
> *Index to Legal Periodicals*
> *Music Index*
> *Reader's Guide to Periodical Literature*
> *Social Science Index*
> *Ulrich's International Periodical Index* (Lists the names of periodicals in many languages. It does not index specific articles.)

Very few newspapers are indexed. It may be possible to find information on world or national events in one of the following newspaper indexes:

Index to the Christian Science Monitor
The New York Times Index
The Times Index, London
The Newspaper Index (indexes a few large American newspapers)

If your library has the material to which the indexes refer, it is probably on microfilm or microfiches.

Local newspapers vary greatly in their manner of filing material about old stories and in their willingness to let people not on staff use the files.

Indexes to Material Shorter Than Book Length

Short works are difficult to locate. They generally come in anthologies. The anthology title does not necessarily indicate what specific works are contained therein. If you want to find a poem, short story, play, or essay, you may find the relevant anthology or anthologies by using an index.

Poetry

Granger's Index to Poetry

Poems are listed by author, first line, title, and subject.

Short Stories

Short Story Index

Short stories are indexed by author, title, and subject. Some periodicals are included, as well as anthologies.

Essays

Essay and General Literature Index

Essays and literary criticism are indexed by author and subject.

Plays

Ottemiller's Index to Plays in Collections, 1900–1975
Indexes plays by author and title.

Play Index (by year)

Bibliographies

Indirectly, you can locate many bibliographies through the card catalog. When you find a book on a subject you are investigating, that book may have a bibliography. No bibliography in a book will be more up-to-date than that book.

Bibliography of Bibliographies   Lists many bibliographies.

Bibliographic Index   Also a bibliography of bibliographies.

Subject Guide to Books in Print   List of American books still in print. The list is arranged by subject and may prove useful as a means of finding titles of books on a particular subject.

Cumulative Books Index   Lists English-language books by subject, author, and title.

There are also many special-subject lists of books. A few examples are:

The Reader's Advisor
Sources of Information in the Social Sciences
Harvard Guide to American History
Science and Engineering Reference Sources

Guides to Finding Books

It is unreasonable to expect any library to carry all the books on every subject. You may have compiled a good bibliography, but then you may not find the books in your library. What do you do?

1. Find out if your library participates in an inter-library loan program. If so, there may be a catalog of the books available on loan from another library.

2. Look it up in *Books in Print*. You will find out if it can be purchased by you or by the library.

3. Try *Paperbound Books in Print*. If you have to buy the books yourself, you may find paperbacks more economical.

4. *Guide to U.S. Government Publications* will provide a list of books available from the U.S. Government Printing Office.

BEYOND THE LIBRARY

The good researcher knows enough to go beyond the library for many kinds of research. Here are some other sources of information:

Other Kinds of Libraries

Company libraries or reference rooms are more likely than a large library to have material on subjects of particular interest to that company's work. If your company does not have at least a reference shelf, it should begin to develop one. At times, you may be able to arrange to use other companies' libraries.

Museum libraries may have highly specialized materials that are helpful. Even a small museum may have a library that is complete in the field of that museum's specialization.

Private libraries may be general or specialized. They may belong to business associations or unions or professional groups. Terms of use differ from one private library to another.

College and university libraries are often for the specific use of faculty and students. Sometimes, however, arrangements can be made by firms or individuals to use the libraries on a regular or temporary basis.

Specialized collections of maps, costumes, recordings, pictures, etc., may be available in your area.

Government and Public Institutions

Try the offices of the city, town, county, or state government. There are many maps, records, and often special information bulletins available.

Government agencies of all levels have a wealth of information. It is up to you to locate the agency and call or write for the information you need.

Chambers of commerce are often glad to supply material and answer questions about their area. They will often direct you to other people or organizations who can supply what they cannot supply.

The federal government's Government Printing Office publishes a large number of pamphlets and books on a tremendous variety of subjects. You can get their Subject Bibliography price list (describing all the Office's publications) or a price list on a specific subject by writing to:

Superintendent of Documents
Government Printing Office
Washington, DC 20402

The following publications are sources of information about the federal government:

Congressional Record. A daily record of the activities of Congress, including indexes giving the names, subjects, and history of all bills.

Official Congressional Directory. Published by the Government Printing Office, a list of the names and addresses of everyone connected with the federal government, maps of Congressional Districts, and short biographies of members of Congress (published annually).

Official Register of the U.S. Government. A list, by agency, of the name, title, salary, and address of all supervisory and administrative personnel of the federal government (published annually).

Private Companies and Agencies

Private companies can supply annual reports—a source of a great deal of economic information. Some libraries have collections of annual reports, but you can also obtain them by writing to the companies.

Private companies are often willing to supply other information about the industry or industries at large.

Large companies often have pamphlets available about basic industrial techniques or products. Some of the material must be evaluated because the companies are trying to maintain a good public image and may not be presenting opposing views.

Private organizations often exist for the purpose of encouraging or discouraging certain practices. They are willing to supply information presenting their point of view. Again, this material must be carefully evaluated because it is often one-sided.

Private agencies and business organizations may have printed information available. For example, the New York Stock Exchange has a great deal of material on the operations of the stock market. Often, such agencies and organizations will answer questions, as well.

Trade Magazines

Most industries have trade magazines that service that industry. Trade magazines have useful articles. They usually put out yearly directories of the companies in that industry, and they may have indexes on the articles published over the year. They may also put out specialized handbooks of interest only to that trade. Most of these trade magazines would not be in a small public library. They may be available on the shelves of businesses in that field. And often back copies can be obtained from the publisher.

Occasionally staff of trade magazines will answer questions or direct you to people who can answer them.

Interviews

Do not ignore the possibility of interviewing people. Some informants may be more reliable than others. You will have to evaluate the information by checking it against what you have learned from other sources.

Alphabetical Key For Quick Reference

9987654321O

FGHIJ-OPM